Dad,
We saw
this book and
thought of you. Had
to send it to you.
Love,
Jeffrey & Heather
May 5, 1987

READY ALL!

George Yeoman Pocock and Crew Racing

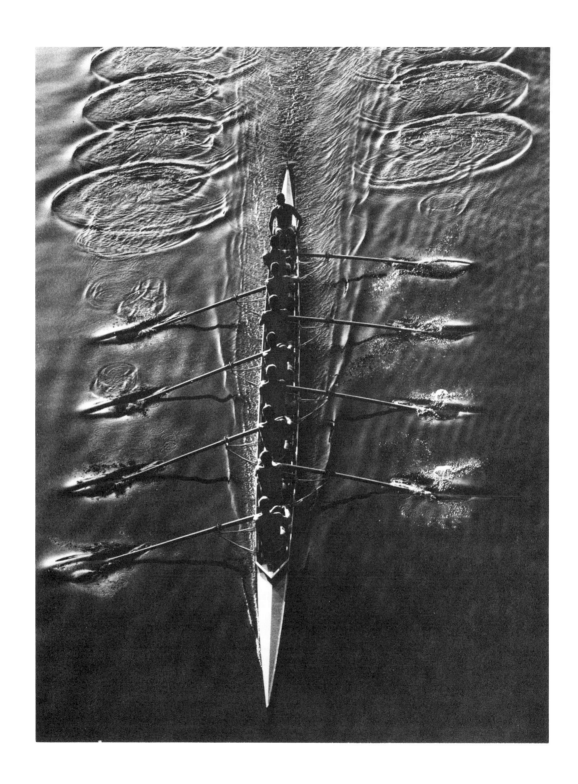

READY ALL!

George Yeoman Pocock and Crew Racing

GORDON NEWELL

Foreword by Dick Erickson

University of Washington Press   *Seattle & London*

Frontispiece by Josef Scaylea

Copyright © 1987 by the University of Washington Press
Manufactured in the United States of America
Composition, printing and binding by Arcata Graphics/Kingsport
Designed by Audrey Meyer

All royalties from this book will go to the Thomas W. McCurdy Memorial Fund,
Board of Rowing Stewards, University of Washington

Library of Congress Cataloging-in-Publication Data

Newell, Gordon R.
Ready all!

Bibliography: p.
Includes index.
1. University of Washington—Rowing—History.
2. Pocock, George Yeoman. I. Title.
GV807.U55N48   1987   797.1′23′071179777   86–27244
ISBN 0–295–96473–1

Contents

Foreword *vii*

Preface *ix*

1. Apprentice Watermen on the Thames *3*

2. Making Do on the Pacific Northwest Frontier *22*

3. Building Shells in the Tokyo Tea Room *34*

4. Building Airplanes at the Red Barn *52*

5. "Clumsily Built Western Boats" *66*

6. "Eight Hearts Must Beat As One" *76*

7. "There Are No Fast Boats, Only Fast Crews" *88*

8. Olympic Gold *100*

9. Races 'round the World *114*

10. Remembered Crews and Coaches *131*

11. The Later Years *145*

Appendixes *160*

Bibliography *171*

Index *173*

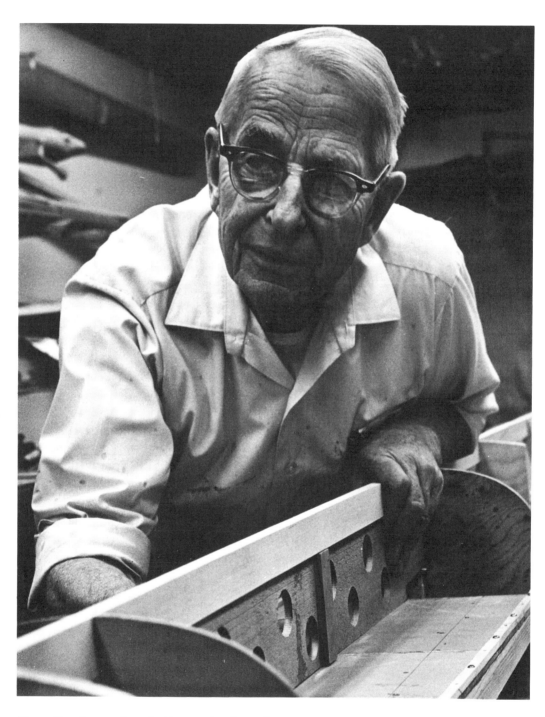

George Pocock at work, early 1970s (photo by Josef Scaylea)

Foreword

"MR. POCOCK." For myself and my classmates, it was always, "Mr. Pocock." I came to the University of Washington as a freshman in the fall of 1954. Being over six feet tall, I was soon escorted to the Conibear Shellhouse by a varsity oarsman to turn out for crew. Coach Stan Pocock assembled the hundred or so freshman and said, "Whether or not you make it or decide to stay with it, in your later years you will always be able to say, 'I rowed at Washington.'" Little did we know how prophetic Stan's words would be.

Washington's reputation, history, and tradition were of course well established by then. Coach (Al) Ulbrickson, Coach (Stan) Pocock, the Conibear Shellhouse, Pocock shells—all were somewhat frightening to the uninitiated freshman. As we went through the fall practices and winter and spring racing, there emerged a person who not only loomed larger but was obviously the connecting link to all this greatness: *Mr. George Pocock.*

Mr. Pocock spoke at our spring crew banquet. He was so humble, so modest. He apologized that growing up at Eton, he was an apprentice boat builder; not being "educated" he felt unqualified to address the alumni and oarsmen. Yet, he was so eloquent, so articulate. He had two messages that night. He spoke of all the rowers over his years, and said that he had "never known one to be a loser in life." His second message was to the varsity crew and he quoted from Shakespeare: "The festering lily smells worse than the ragweed." Powerful messages . . . subtle messages that Mr. Pocock constantly imparted to the oarsman.

His favorite athletes were those who struggled in the third or fourth shells. He welcomed the athletes to his shop to discuss rowing, but we soon learned that if he was steaming a fresh cedar plank or carving a bow stem for a new eight, we'd better come back later. He would often watch the crew as they left the dock and as they returned two hours later. He didn't ride in the coaching launch very often, but when he did everyone tried even harder. In discussions, he knew exactly how everyone rowed. He didn't tell you how to row—he was a master at having you question and analyze your own rowing. But above all, after a few moments with Mr. Pocock, you felt better about your rowing and, most important, about yourself.

It took time to appreciate the Pocock racing shell. As one learns to row, and we are always learning, the fine subtleties of matching wood with athletes emerge. There is a specific purpose for not only each piece of wood, but for its source and its shape. It is all designed to be useful, helpful, and, yes, aesthetic. Mr. Pocock felt all these qualities were necessary to help the oarsman achieve his fullest potential.

To know the man, to strive in his artistic presentation of the rowing shell, to listen to his stories, and speeches, to watch him row his single, to observe his influence on others, to have been selected by him to pursue a coaching career, is an honor for which I will always be grateful.

On behalf of all the oarsmen and coaches who had the privilege of knowing George Pocock, I would like to thank H. W. McCurdy and Gordon Newell for making this wonderful man's life story a permanent part of the history of modern competitive rowing.

Dick Erickson
Varsity Crew Coach
University of Washington

Preface

This story of George Yeoman Pocock is also the story of amateur rowing throughout much of the twentieth century, for the man, his craftsmanship, and his total dedication to the sport had a profound influence upon it. He brought the design and building of the racing shell to its ultimate perfection, and although he had many imitators, he had no peers.

A champion oarsman himself, he unobtrusively and modestly imparted his technical skills to young men who, as crew coaches at universities across the nation, have passed on his teachings in later years to new generations of young athletes involved in what he proudly proclaimed "the last truly amateur sport."

Probably most important of all was his Socratic influence on the sport. He evolved and preached the philosophy of competitive rowing as a source of strength, character, and total dedication; an unselfish dedication, he said, for there were no athletic scholarships, no lucrative professional contracts, not even individual stardom. The reward was the joy in achieving the perfect team effort which, when achieved, "approaches the divine." An inspirational speaker, he lifted the hearts and spirits— and the pride—of young oarsmen all across America.

Although many of those he influenced are no longer young athletes, they have not forgotten George Pocock and, indeed, they made this book possible.

The bases for this book are the memoirs of George Pocock, written by him in his later years at the behest of H. W. McCurdy, and a large collection of ephemera, including newspaper clippings and photographs, magazine articles, inscribed photographs, correspondence with coaches, oarsmen, and other members of the rowing fraternity, and other items, some relating to his early years in England. With typical modesty, George had indicated that he did not feel his memoirs would be of historical interest, and Mr. McCurdy was delighted to learn that he had in fact taken the proposal seriously, and that his typescript was included in the large amount of written and pictorial material preserved by the Pocock family and turned over to the writer by his son Stan. The suggestion made years ago by his close friend was the genesis of this book, for without the Pocock memoirs, it could not have been written. And a most significant chapter in the history and philosophy of an ancient and honorable sport would have been lost, and perhaps eventually forgotten.

H. W. McCurdy, who rowed at both Washington and MIT, provided the grant for its research and writing, and provided much historical material. Stan Pocock, oarsman and coach at Washington, and other members of the Pocock family have been most cooperative, providing invaluable material and photographs. Robert G. Moch, coxswain of Washington's Olympic Gold Medal crew of 1936 and now a Seattle attorney, read the manuscript, correcting errors and adding information. Similar assistance was provided by Arthur E. Campbell, also a varsity coxswain (under Hiram Conibear in 1912) and also a Seattle attorney, and by Gordon Callow, another former crewman and the son of legendary Coach Rusty Callow. Further support and assistance were provided by Hunter Simpson, former crewman and presently chairman of the University Board of Regents, and by present Washington crew coach Dick Erickson.

Harry Arlett, with the Regatta headquarters at Henley-on-Thames, Oxfordshire, England, was most helpful in supplying photographs and additional information. Mr. Arlett, who first met George Pocock at the Berlin Olympics in 1936, adds this interesting sidelight on Pocock's early sculling career, and that of his brother, Dick: "I have in my possession a Silver Sculling Shield, open to all scullers, which was won by R. J. (Dick) Pocock in 1909, and by George in 1910."

He adds that the most impressive compliment to Pocock craftsmanship in his experience was the efforts by British rowing authorities to buy the Pocock-built shells of American crews, "who always seemed to win" in the early post–World War II years. On one occasion, he writes, "to the best of my recollection, it happened to be the University of Washington, and although they were not keen to part with their shell, they were eventually persuaded to do so."

Gordon Newell
September 1986

READY ALL!

George Yeoman Pocock and Crew Racing

It's a great art, is rowing
It's the finest art there is.
It's a symphony of motion.
And when you're rowing well
Why it's nearing perfection.
And when you reach perfection
You're touching the divine.
It touches the you of you's
Which is your soul.

George Pocock

Mair

1

Apprentice Watermen on the Thames

THE RACING of oar-powered boats as both an amateur and professional sport in England can be traced back to the early eighteenth century. When American colleges began adding crew to their list of major sports around the middle of the last century, it was natural that pioneering American oarsmen should turn to British veterans for guidance.

American rowing enthusiasts like Bob Cook crossed the Atlantic to view the long-established programs of English clubs, colleges, and prep schools. British oarsmen like Rudy Lehmann or Guy Nickalls were brought over to advise and instruct their American counterparts. But the greatest and most lasting influence on the sport in America came from two young English watermen just out of apprenticeship as boat-builders and racing scullers on the placid waters of the River Thames. George and Dick Pocock cherished no dreams of becoming legendary figures in the annals of American rowing when they voyaged by steerage from London to Halifax with a few dollars in their pockets. The year was 1911, there were no jobs for them in England, and they had heard that an able-bodied man could make ten dollars a day sawing down trees in British Columbia.

Until they overheard the chance remark about the rich rewards of tree-cutting in western Canada, the Pocock boys had planned to seek their fortunes in Australia or New Zealand, so it might be said they came to America by accident, but they remained by choice, and by so doing, they profoundly enriched the boats, rig, style, and rowing techniques of the sport in America.

More important, perhaps, George became an inspiring voice in the building of

George Pocock's grandfather and father at the entrance of the elder Pocock's London pub, the Albion, which he operated after retiring as a boatbuilder. Photo probably taken in the 1880s.

pride and *esprit* in the young athletes who manned the beautiful craft he and his brother built for them. Although he had no formal schooling beyond the age of fourteen, George was an omnivorous reader and he was steeped in the traditions of generations of watermanship. He came to be called to colleges across the nation to speak at major rowing events, and what he had to say was truly inspirational. His came to be the guiding philosophy of what Rowing Hall of Famer H. W. McCurdy proudly calls the last true amateur major sport in American universities.

Since there are no fat scholarships for oarsmen, no million dollar contracts for professionals, and because they function as teams without individual stars, they truly epitomize the lines of Rudyard Kipling: "And no one shall work for the money, / And no one shall work for fame."

George had the knack of putting that spirit into words, and of making his young listeners quietly proud to be a part of it.

The Pocock boys were born into a family of skilled boatbuilders. Their grandfather Pocock had been a Thames-side boatbuilder until he made enough money to realize the dream of many English workingmen and seamen. He opened a pub, the Albion, in London. Their maternal grandfather Vicars was a master of the same trade, having spent seven years in Germany in charge of a crew of English boatbuilders constructing the first racing shells in that country. Doughty Grandpa Vicars admitted that during his seven years in the Fatherland the only German word he learned was "Ja."

George recalled that "Grandpa Vicars was a rugged customer, physically very strong. He won a track race for veterans over fifty years of age when he was past seventy. The prize was a walking stick, which he threw or gave away."

The boys' father, Aaron Pocock, plied his trade of boatbuilding with the same artistry he devoted to his avocation of portrait painting, but he certainly was not a hard-headed businessman. He had served his apprenticeship under his father-in-law at Kingston-on-Thames, a couple of miles above Teddington Lock where the river becomes tidal, and about twelve miles from Eton, where the boys would spend most of their youth.

He opened his own business there. The boats he produced were much admired, but he was given to risking his hard-earned profits on such ill-fated ventures as a device designed to speed up and simplify the operation of wherries, the small, one-man rowing boats which took the place of taxis on the Thames at London.

George recalled that "a man had invented a mechanism for a person to sit in the stem of a boat and pump the machine with his arms or legs. The machine was connected with a propeller which drove the boat along instead of using oars. Dad financed it, and it broke him. He went to an uncle, Fred Pocock, in Cambridge, who was building boats and prospering, to make a touch. He was refused, at which Dad, who was a great believer in family loyalty as well as a good boxer, gave him one on the chin, thus ending the family relationship there."

To the further detriment of his business, Aaron's friends kept bringing him photographs of their loved ones from which they asked him to paint portraits. Kind-hearted Aaron could bring himself neither to refuse, nor to accept any payment for the result of a couple of days' work on the canvas.

Finally a former fellow apprentice named Bob Porter was set up by his well-to-do parents in a rival boatbuilding business just across the river. Also, by the 1890s, steam launches were gaining popularity on the river and, along with the bicycle craze ashore, limiting the demand for the traditional rowing boats.

Both Aaron and his erstwhile friend across the river went bankrupt.

George was born at Kingston on March 23, 1891, the fourth child of Aaron and his first wife, the former Lucy Vicars. His brother Dick was two years older, and there were two older sisters, Julia and Lucy. Their mother died when George was six months old, and when he was four, Aaron married Margaret Watts, who died giving birth to the last Pocock daughter, Kathleen.

So it was that, following his business failure and with five small children to raise alone, Aaron was forced to take a step down in life, from proprietor of his own enterprise to journeyman worker. And in those days and in that trade, journeyman meant just that. He had to journey up and down the Thames wherever he could find work.

"He was a very sad man," his youngest son wrote. "He never told us much, but we too sensed his grief, and were usually considerate of his feelings. The only words he ever told me of my mother were many years later, when my wife Frances and I visited him in Battersea, London, returning from the Berlin Olympic Games of 1936, and his words then were, 'Your mother was a good woman.' And I have no doubt she was. She was a graduate of the London Royal Academy of Music, and played the organ in the Kingston church where her father, good old Grandpa Vicars, held the honorary post of Verger. She was also the village music teacher, and Dad's sister was one of her pupils, which is probably how he met her."

Their bereaved father was often away from home, and the children were largely raised by a series of housekeepers. Aaron couldn't afford much in the way of wages, and five active and sometimes quarrelsome children were a handful. There were seven housekeepers over the three or four years until George was nine and his sister Lucy, at thirteen, took over the household duties. George remembered only one of the surrogate mothers, a Mrs. Shepherd, with affection. "She must have been like a mother would be to her son," he recalled. "She darned my stockings, saw that I was clean, trimmed my hair and, above everything else, taught me a prayer and told me of the love of Jesus. I would go off to school in high glee, feeling the equal of every other boy. Mrs. Shepherd was a devout churchwoman, and to this day I remember being with her in church, the only one of the five."

Under such conditions the lives of the Pocock children might well have been melancholy, but George didn't remember them that way. His recollections provide a charming picture of nineteenth-century family life and childhood activities along the tranquil reaches of the Thames:

"My father's sister, Aunt Julia, was also widowed, with five children about our ages and, like us, two boys and three girls. At Christmas time our tribe would go up to Aunt Julia's home at Brookley on the outskirts of London, and there we would celebrate the Christmas season. What glorious times those were. I have never seen Dad so happy. He would dance with his sister and show us how to do a schottish. We would all sit around a big table and play 'Banker' with nuts for money. Dad always ended up with all the 'money' . . . and always used the occasion as warning to us never to gamble with real money: you're sure to lose."

Years before, Grandma Pocock had taken an orphan boy named George Colbert to raise. Although never formally adopted, he had come to be regarded as a member of the family. To all the children he was "Uncle George," and they regarded him with awe as a truly heroic figure. He had enlisted in the Royal Navy as a youth and had risen to highest petty officer rank. He was often at the family Christmas festivities and held the children spellbound with sailors' hornpipes and sea chanties sung in a grand voice. On one occasion, George recalled, "Uncle George" arrived late—on Boxing Day, December 26. "He said he had been with his ship to the west coast of Africa to put down an uprising of the natives. With eyes like saucers, I asked, 'Did you have to kill anybody, Uncle George?.' 'No,' he replied. 'We sent the demolition squad ashore and they blew up a couple of mahogany trees. The rebels came crawling out of the bush and surrendered on the spot.' That part of Africa now is the independent nation of Ghana."

"And then," George recalled, "there was the Christmas dinner: turkey and a big ham and all the fixings. After dinner all the kids would go out caroling, taking along a box for donations to Dr. Barnado's Home for Orphaned Children, and come back with it heavy with coins. Oh what a joy it all was!"

It was always a wondrous occasion too when old Grandpa Vicars came to visit. He had many yarns to spin, but the one that impressed young George the most was his grandfather's association with H. M. Stanley, who had been sent to search for the famous African missionary and explorer, David Livingston, in 1871. George recalled the story in later years:

> Stanley came to London to outfit for his journey to central Africa in search of Livingston. Stanley visited the boatbuilding firm of Messengers, where Grandpa Vicars was superintendent. He wanted them to build him a boat which would come apart in small enough pieces to be carried by native bearers, and could be bolted together when needed to carry a dozen people. Grandpa Vicars was given the job of designing and building it, and he used to delight in explaining to us kids how he went about it. He always licked the palm of his left hand, rubbed his hands together, and started in.
>
> He built a clinker boat of six lapstrakes, fitted thick two-inch bulkheads about every three feet, sawed them around to make a frame roughly two by four inches, fastened them to the planking with wood screws a half inch from each edge. Then he drilled bolt holes through these frames every three inches, and when all this was done, he took a cross-cut saw and cut the boat into pieces through these frames. When it was all in pieces, the bolts were inserted to put it back together—and presto!—one of the first portable boats ever made.

Grandpa Pocock died before the boys came to know him, but his two brothers, William and Thomas, sometimes put in an appearance to tell them of other aspects of river boating. They were both professional scullers, racing other single-oared boats for cash wagers. Bill was also rowing coach at Westminster, a well-known prep school. The coach had to pull stroke oar and coach at the same time, since no power launch of those days could keep pace with a well-rowed shell. [1]

Long before they were old enough to leave school and become apprentice boatbuilders, the Pocock boys were thus steeped in the lore of racing boats and the intense competition which breathed life and meaning into them.

During those early years, the Pocock children lived in the village of Shepperton on Thames, where their father's steadiest work was at Dunton's boat shop. The family occupied a small house known locally as "the Cottage," which had what seemed to the children a very large fruit orchard adjoining it. One of George's earliest recollections is of his father standing at the gate giving apples to the schoolchildren as they passed by.

George retained unpleasant memories of the small and ancient church on Shepperton Green, which he attended with the motherly Mrs. Shepherd. Years later, on the

---

1. Rowing as a sport began at prep schools long before the universities took it up. The first chronicled race between Westminister and Eton was in 1811. The first recorded race between Oxford and Cambridge universities was not until 1828.

return trip from the Berlin Olympics via England, he revisited the church at Shepperton and discovered why his childhood religious devotions had caused him such discomfort:

> As a child it was agony to sit through a sermon. No wonder. Those old pew seats, I realized, had sloped downward at an angle, so the congregation had to sit up ramrod straight with no support for their backs. I suppose this was designed to keep people from dozing off during the sermons, but the result was much physical as well as mental suffering, particularly for children. Fortunately, there were a lot of faded old battle flags hanging from the church rafters, and I was able to get some relief from my physical discomfort by gazing upward piously and losing myself in fantasies of brave soldiers on horseback tearing into the enemy ranks with those banners flying. I was glad, on behalf of a new generation of Shepperton children, to find that, in 1936, the old pews had been replaced by new ones more fitted to the human body.

Before George was ten years old, he escaped the bodily torments of the old Shepperton church. His father was offered a permanent position as boatbuilder at Eton College, one of England's most venerable and prestigious prep schools.[2] Its headmaster, Dr. Edmund Warre, was launching an extensive program of rowing as a means of diverting some of the overabundant energies of 1,100 healthy youths from thirteen to seventeen years of age. Strenuous physical activity was an integral part of the Eton regimen—cross country running and indoor gymnastics in the winter, cricket, rowing, and sculling in the spring and summer. So popular were the last two sports that Dr. Warre had set a goal of 650 boats. Aaron was one of the four-man crew working to build up the fleet to that level over a period of several years.

It was a step up for him from the status of self-employed journeyman to a regular job at assured pay. And it was to lead to even better things, for a while at any rate.

The Pocock family moved the few miles up the Thames to the twin towns of Eton and Windsor, separated only by a bridge across the river. Both are rich in history and tradition: Eton is famous for its fifteenth-century college, and Windsor for its ancient castle, construction of which was begun by William the Conqueror in 1066. George was told that the cherished name of Windsor is derived from the river that flows beneath its towers: "Standing on top of the castle's round tower, you have a sweeping view of the countryside and the winding river. From this view came the name, Winds-'oer, now Windsor."

2. Eton College was established in the fifteenth century by King Henry VI as the "King's College for Our Lady of Eton beside Windsor," especially for boys of gentle birth whose parents could not afford an upper-class education for them, usually the sons of poorly paid vicars and curates of poorer parishes. Enrollment was originally limited to 100, but in the sixteenth century it was opened to paying students, although to this day 100 scholarships are still awarded.

Even at the turn of the century, when the Pocock family arrived, boating was an ancient tradition with the boys of Eton. At the time of the American Revolution they were racing in the college boats and staging boat parades on the river to commemorate the birthday of King George III.

The boatbuilders on Aaron's crew worked on a piecework basis—so much for an eight-oared shell, less on a graduated scale for the smaller boats: fours, pairs, and singles.[3] Aaron was not only a skilled and efficient boatbuilder, but was spurred on by debts incurred during his years in the uncertain trade of journeyman. As a result, he not only turned out the best boats, but he did it a lot faster than his mates. He was warned that he must "ease up." He was earning too much money.

But in 1903, when it came time for the manager of the Eton boathouse to retire, Aaron's skill and hard work paid off. The retiring manager, a Mr. Manard, strongly recommended Pocock to E. L. Churchill, a college master who was Dr. Warre's advocate for rowing. Manard took Churchill to the boatshop, where he introduced him to Aaron, saying, "This is the man I must recommend. He is the best worker and he does the best work."

Churchill shook hands with the craftsman and said, "I appoint you as the new manager."

"And that, I think, was the first real break in Dad's life," George observed. "Dad being general manager gave us privileges we did not have before, such as taking a boat and going for a row on the river. I was twelve years old on this occasion of Dad's rise up in the world. The 'rise up,' as I put it, must be understood not in a large salary by any means, but in comparative economic security and standing in the community."

Free education in England at that time ended at the age of fourteen. George Pocock had entered the one-room, one-teacher "infant school" on Shepperton Green at the age of five. One of his most vivid early memories was of the school festivities in 1897 in observance of Queen Victoria's Diamond Jubilee Year:

> All the children had what we called a "tea-fight and bun-struggle" at the school, and were each presented with a porcelain mug with the Queen's picture on it and a threepenny coin inside. We got our first lesson in the wicked ways of the world when we were let out. A merry-go-round had been set up on the green opposite the school and we ran over to take a ride at a penny a ride. But the proprietor refused to give us change, so we

---

3. Another example of the deep roots of rowing in British history is the evolution of the "rowing eight," or eight-oared shell, as the standard for major crew racing events worldwide. Tradition has it that the eight-man crews honored the ancient kings of England, whose royal barges were rowed by eight watermen.

had to stay on for three rides, and there went my three pence: the most money I had ever handled. My sense of fair play was shocked, and I assured myself that if my Dad had been there he would have taken the scheming merry-go-round man to task in no uncertain terms.

George later attended the free school at Eton taught by a Mr. Machin. During Christmas festivities one year, the children picked up a catchy tune sung between choruses with an endless series of jingles. When school resumed on Monday morning, one of the more daring students began the popular ditty. When Mr. Machin entered, the entire student body was in full voice on one of the jingles:

> There was a young lady of Eton,
> A figure with plenty of meat on.
> Marry me Mac and find on my back,
> A place to warm your cold feet on.

The words seem innocuous today, but Mr. Machin was scandalized. He rushed up and down in front of the student body waving his cane and shouting for silence. Drowned out by the rollicking chorus, he began whacking singers with his cane until the singing faltered and died out.

Grandpa Vicars was confirmed in his belief that discipline in the British schoolroom wasn't what it used to be. He informed George that when *he* had been in school, the master would start every day by whacking every boy over the head with a leather scabbard, just in case he missed any youthful misdemeanors later in the day.

At fourteen, George sat for a scholarship at the London Polytechnic School, a teacher training institution. He missed winning it by one point, and his formal education ended with commencement exercises at which each graduate was presented with two books: the Bible and Church of England Prayer Book in one volume, and the works of Shakespeare. They were admonished to digest these volumes thoroughly. They would then have a grasp of all the literature they would ever need. George did indeed study them avidly, but they were only the first of a library of books he collected and devoured over the years. And he remained convinced that the nine years of concentrated education he received in England provided the equivalent of at least a present-day high school course.

With the doors to further formal education thus closed to him, George was indentured to his father for five years as an apprentice boatbuilder at Eton.

For about a month before the apprenticeship began, he worked at the college bookstore of Spottiswood & Company, making change for the few cash purchases and keeping careful invoices of the large number of transactions made on credit—"on tick" in the argot of Eton. It was also his duty to carefully inscribe the names of all subscribers on the paper wrappers of the London daily papers and the weekly and monthly magazines. His hours were six in the morning to six at night; his pay six shillings a week. And young George Pocock hated every minute of it. The smell of the river, the sight of the darting boats and the coxswains' cries of "Ready All!" as the oarsmen prepared to swing into action made his humdrum bookstore tasks intolerable.

It was with a vast sense of relief that he reported to his father at the boatbuilding shop. "What a contrast in enjoyment," he reflected in later years. "To me the change was nothing less than heavenly."

Even the menial tasks to which he was assigned at first—sweeping up the shop and learning to sharpen tools—he performed with pride and delight. He was involved, however humbly, in the building of boats, and it was clear to him that he had entered upon his true vocation.

"There were absolutely no power tools, no machinery of any kind," he recalled. "Everything was done by hand, and to me the smell of the wood was sweeter than any perfume: Norway pine for the stringers, white ash for ribs and shoulders, and Spanish cedar for the skin and washboards."

Gradually George mastered the art of sawing and hand planing, and he eagerly absorbed the knowledge and skills of his father and the other master boatbuilders. Nor was his intimacy with the boats limited to learning the techniques of their building. By the time he began his apprenticeship, he had been sculling a single for two years, and he was becoming very good at it.

"My father put me in a single shell when I was twelve years old," he recalled, "and I took to sculling very readily. I rowed my first race when I was fifteen, a junior race in the Henley on Thames town regatta, and won it."

George thus had an early taste of competitive rowing at Henley, the shrine and goal of amateur oarsmen around the free world. He continued in his memoirs:

> At the age of seventeen, Dad entered me in a professional race at Putney on Thames, which is really just a suburb of London. It was a handicap race based on the then professional champion of the world, Ernest Barry, as scratch. There were fifty-eight entries. Dad said, "Now you can build your own boat for this race, and I will give you one bit of advice. No one will ask how long it took you to build it, they will only ask *who* built it." That was his way of saying, "Take your time. Do it right," which I did.
>
> Dad laid out the plan for me and I went to work. There was an old sixteen-foot-long 3 × 12 Norway pine plank kicking around the shop and I kept thinking what a fine skin it would make for my shell if I could get smaller planks sawn from it. I asked Dad

Certificate awarded George Pocock, along with a prize, as winner of junior sculling championship at London, 1907

about it, and he sent it to a mill in London, and fourteen planks came back as though they had been planed. The sawing was far superior to what is done today. I planked my single with this Norway pine, and in contrast to the white skin I put mahogany washboards on. It made it very distinctive, because all the other boats at Eton had reverse color scheme; dark Spanish cedar or mahogany skins and white washboards. The finished product really looked super.

My brother Dick and I rowed our singles down river to the town of Barnes four miles above Putney Bridge. We kept them there at a boathouse owned by Tommy Green, a friend of Dad's. We stayed there two weeks, spending most of the time in continued training for the race. Since I was two years younger than Dick, I had a better handicap and therefore a better chance of winning. The race course was from Hammersmith to Putney, a distance of two miles. Most of the fifty-eight contestants were eliminated in the early heats, which finished on a Saturday. I was one of the four finalists for the final heat, which was to be rowed on Monday.

I had contracted a severe cold during race week, but I tried to ignore it, and did so to a great extent. I nursed it all day Sunday. First prize was fifty pounds sterling, a huge sum to me in those days, and I was determined to win it.

On Monday Dick and I took the train for Barnes, where we picked up our boats and dropped down to Hammersmith for the start of the final race. The other three contenders were Charles Harding, former champion of England; John Bowton, a big twenty-six-year-old red headed policeman from Hackney, the toughest district of London; and Billy Coles from Erith, below London Bridge. I had to give Bowton and Coles a two second start, and I received two seconds from Harding. My dad gave me some advice at the start of the race. He said, "Now Wag Harding knows this course blindfolded. He has lived on it. Be sure and keep him directly astern and you will not have to keep looking around to see if you are on course."

The race started, with Bowton and Coles off first, then me, and four seconds later, Harding. I caught Coles in about a mile, and soon after passed Bowton, with Harding astern from the start. Then Bowton began to overhaul me. He was very strong, but not a really expert sculler; a bit sloppy. I glued my eyes on my boat's stern, with an occasional glance at Harding to fix my course, and really went to work. I reached the finish line almost neck-and-neck with Bowton. I wasn't sure whether I had won or not until Bowton looked over at me and said, "You won." I had beaten him by less than a boat's length.

I paddled back to Putney boathouse a mighty happy kid. Dad was beaming too, as he helped me out of the boat. He whispered, "Two weeks ago I put five pounds on you at twenty to one odds." His confidence in me had paid off to the tune of a hundred pounds sterling.

The sponsors of the race, *The Sportsman* newspaper, had a representative there, who handed me my winner's check for fifty pounds, which I viewed as a small fortune. The next morning's issue of the paper described the race, adding, "Young Pocock was undoubtedly aided by the excellent ship he utilized." They didn't say who built it, but that didn't matter. I knew.

Aaron also pointed out oarsmen worthy of emulation:

Dad was a keen student of rowing and sculling, and he always said that the then champion sculler of the world, Ernest Barry, was the best he had ever seen: a true artist. He often sent me down to Putney to watch carefully how Barry did it. He told me if I could learn to duplicate Ernie's style I would continue to win races.

One afternoon I was sitting on the bank when Barry came in to the float and sang out, "Hey, kid. Do you want to try my boat?" Did I! It was like Babe Ruth asking an American boy if he wanted to try out his bat. I wasted no time in shoving off in his boat, the *Gertrude Sharlotte* (named after his wife). I sculled up the river about half a mile and by the time I got back he was dressed and waiting for me on the float . . . and he asked *me* how I liked the boat. I replied "very much indeed, but your sculls are heavier than mine at home." He told me he had them especially made that way because he wanted to tire quickly to get his second wind early. "Then I can go forever," he explained.

Dad was very proud of his offspring and their rowing ability. Even young Lucy was a skilled oarswoman, and my brother Richard was a splendid physical specimen, nearly six feet five in his bare feet. He won many races, the most important being Doggett's Coat and Badge, the oldest recorded rowing competition in history. Thomas Doggett was a successful London actor in the early eighteenth century, and like most Londoners, he took passage from one point of the city to another in the Thames River "taxi" boats, favoring the small, fast wherries operated by a single boatman, and he always offered extra money if his boatman could outrun the other boats in the vicinity.

These Thames watermen so intrigued him that he put a sum of money in trust with the Crown-chartered Company of Fishmongers to pay for the prize of distinctive coat and badge and ten pounds prize money for winners of a five-mile race from London Bridge to Chelsea. Notices of the first race were posted on August 1, 1715, to commemorate the accession to the Throne of the House of Hanover in the person of George I. Contestants were limited to young watermen in the final year of their apprenticeship. It was also stipulated that regular water traffic was not be be stopped for the race. That made it a true test of watermanship, for the course covered the busiest area of the crowded river, with the wakes of passing ships setting up a great deal of turbulence.

George helped his brother train for the event on home waters at Eton, rowing ten miles a day as hard as they could go. Two weeks before the race, they sculled down the river the thirty-five miles from Eton to London Bridge. They stored their boats with an ancient river mariner, a friend of their father's, who had a shack practically under the bridge. Thereafter they commuted daily to practice sculling in the heavy traffic and rough water of the legendary racecourse. George admitted that it was "a scary experience," but they soon got used to it and "handled it well."

Their father held the ancient title of Bargemaster to the Company of Fishmongers, then mainly an honorary one with the single duty of acting as starter and umpire of the Doggett's Coat and Badge Race, a function he had performed for some forty years. It required all his experience and skill to control the start at London Bridge, with the teeming boat and ship traffic of the river going about its business as if nothing unusual were happening. A false start couldn't be called back, because the tide was running fast. The six competing shells were held in place by stake boats, and it had been found impossible to start them by megaphone, for as soon as the starter lifted it they were off. A starting gun didn't work either. When the starter's arm began to move, the eager scullers headed downstream. Aaron had finally evolved a workable system. He would hide behind the pilot house of his launch, and the launch skipper would tell him when everything was in readiness. Then he would dash out at top speed and wave the flag. That worked, and when the flag appeared, the race started. Dick Pocock was in the lead from the start, and he was never headed. At the grand banquet at Fishmongers' Hall after the race, he was escorted past a

THE WATERMAN'S DERBY.

Aaron Pocock, in the livery of Bargemaster of the Fishmongers' Company, prepares to start a race for Doggett's Coat and Badge from London Bridge to Chelsea, 1910. Dick Pocock, who wins the race, is shown at lower right (London Daily Graphic *photo*).

guard of honor composed of winners of years past, to receive the livery and badge prescribed by Thomas Doggett two centuries earlier.

In earlier times, the distinctive livery had been a great business asset to the Thames boatmen who wore it. It marked them as the very best, and their services were much in demand. Things had changed, but it was still a great mark of prestige within the rowing fraternity, and George was looking forward to 1911 when, as a final year apprentice, he would be eligible to compete. But fate had other things in store for him.

The years between 1903 and 1910 were idyllic ones for the entire Pocock family.

ANOTHER WATERWOMEN'S RACE.

MISS POCOCK AGAIN BEATS MISS BRADY.

George's sister Lucy wins the women's sculling match on the Thames at London, 1910 (London Daily Mirror *photo*).

One of the four-oared practice shells at Eton was used for family rowing excursions on Sunday evenings. Older sister Julia pulled stroke oar, Lucy next, Dick at number 2, George at bow, with youngest sister Kathleen at the coxswain's tiller and Aaron, as skipper, directing from the stern. All the family, girls as well as boys, pulled their weight like veterans. (Lucy won the women's championship of England, sculling her single in the 1910 race sponsored by the *London Daily Mirror*.) They challenged and always beat the river steamers, to the delight of the shell's skipper and crew, and the steamboats' passengers.

To George, who possessed a deep interest in history and literature, the surroundings of his boyhood were a constant delight. He joined with his brother and other youths for active sports which included, in addition to rowing, bicycle racing, swimming, and hunting. But he often made solitary pilgrimages to places of ancient legend and quiet beauty which were of little interest to the other lads.

Sometimes he would scull the seven miles downriver to the island of Runnymede, the tiny spot of green on the bosom of the Thames where, in 1215, the barons of England forced King John to sign the Magna Carta, building the foundation of rights still exercised by free men everywhere. Across the river he would walk the green expanse of Egham Mede, where the knights and their men-at-arms assembled to show their force and determination to the reluctant king.

A favorite walk was to the nearby tiny village of Stoke Poges and the quiet churchyard where the eighteenth-century British poet Thomas Gray wrote his "Elegy in a Country Churchyard." Standing in the shade of the great yew tree under which Gray sat and wrote, and which sheltered his grave, young George remembered the haunting lines of the "Elegy." He still remembered them six decades later, though to him Windsor was so central to his recollections that he always lengthened the first line to "The curfew *from Windsor Castle* tolls the knell of parting day."

He also witnessed the pageantry of history in the making as the crowned heads of pre–World War I Europe paraded up to Windsor Castle for Queen Victoria's funeral, the coronation of Edward VII in 1902, and Edward's funeral seven years later. When the Eton Fire Brigade, of which the Pocock brothers were members, was lined up in full uniform to hold back the crowds, Dick towered so high in his brass helmet that the German Kaiser stopped in amazement to inspect him, perhaps reflecting that he would make a splendid addition to his Imperial Guard.

The association between the hardworking sons of the master boatbuilder and the privileged students of Eton was an amiable one. The Pocock boys were admired and respected by the youthful aristocrats for their athletic prowess and boating skills. In such a water-oriented milieu as Eton, watermanship was a great equalizer. The Pocock brothers were well liked by the boys of Eton, some of whom weren't above asking their help in improving their skills.

Among those they coached was a youth named Anthony Eden, scion of a centuries-old baronial family, who would leave Eton to join the army in 1914 and rise to the rank of brigade major at the age of twenty. He went on to become a cabinet officer under Winston Churchill, and later Prime Minister of England. They built singles for a couple of very highly placed lads, Prince Prajadipok of Siam and Lord Grosvenor, the son of the Duke of Westminister. Prajadipok was to become the last of the absolute monarchs of Siam (now Thailand). When the shells were finished, George and Dick taught their royal proteges how to handle them. They did the same for future merchant princes and distinguished scientists—young Mr. Holt of the Blue Funnel Steamship family, young Mr. Cunard of the Cunard Line, and a stout lad named J. B. S. Haldane, who always seemed to be deep in thought. He exasperated his young coaches when, after taking a few strokes with his oars, he would stop, incline his chin on his chest and continue his cogitations, oblivious of his surroundings. He became Britain's leading biochemist and geneticist.

Holt was even more portly than the budding scientist. So much so, in fact, that the Pocock brothers had to build him a special, extra-wide, shallow-draft shell, which was christened by the other boys "Holt's War Punt."

Moderate drinking was not banned by the masters of Eton. Presumably it was felt that part of the training of a British gentleman entailed the ability to hold his liquor gracefully. There was even an approved pub, the Christopher Top in the village, where the teen-age students were permitted to refresh themselves. But overindulgence was cause for expulsion.

Young Cunard, George recalled, did go overboard on one occasion. The biggest event of the year at Eton was Founders' Day, June 4, when the parents came to visit. After a play and speeches by the students, a marine parade led to Lord Desborough's house, where a banquet was held, complete with champagne. The parade consisted of broad-beamed practice eights with battleship-like names such as *Britannia, Dreadnaught,* and *Thetis,* led by a big ten-oared boat named *Monarch.* Dr. Warre had ordained that, on the return voyage, the boys should stand at attention and remove their hats as they passed the reviewing stand containing their parents. He no doubt hoped that this requirement would result in less pre-race tippling, for sobriety is essential to standing at attention in a racing shell.

Cunard, moved either by excess champagne or by the excitement of the occasion, stood on the gunwale of *Britannia,* causing it to capsize spectacularly. Dick and George sped out in a big punt and rescued all hands, depositing them dripping on shore.

George admitted later that their heroics were unnecessary, since all the boys of the *Britannia* were excellent swimmers.

All in all, those years at Eton were golden ones for the Pocock brothers. In short, a "blessing" as George looked back on "Dad's job."

But they ended late in 1910. Aaron lost his job, a victim of staff rivalries and politics. Mr. Churchill, the rowing master, gave him the news sadly. They had become warm friends and the teacher, who had recently come into a large fortune, offered to buy the boathouses and the entire boat fleet and turn them over to Aaron, to be paid for over a period of years from student fees. Finding that the principal riverfront boating structure, which had stood for four hundred years, was in imminent danger of collapse, Aaron considered the potential liability and declined the offer.

His two sons, tremendously popular with the students, were asked to stay on, but their loyalty to their father precluded that. The dispirited Pocock family moved to another small town, West Drayton, about seven miles from Eton. Aaron had received a small bequest from Grandma Pocock, who had died in London, and he pooled resources with two friends to open a "very modest" motion picture theater. After managing it for a short time, a disillusioned Aaron talked his associates into buying him out and went back to itinerant boatbuilding.

It proved to be a crossroads for the close-knit family. George recalled:

Dick and I tried hard for jobs around London, but no luck at all. So it had to be the colonies for us, but which . . . Canada? New Zealand? Australia? We decided on Australia because we knew that rowing was a popular sport there.

A few days before we were to go up to London to book our passage, a flame of Lucy's called at the house in West Drayton. His bowler hat was bashed in and his suit was covered with thorns and brush as though he had fallen into a hedge. This young man's name was Charlie Young, and he was plainly full of Dutch courage; probably planning to pop the question to Lucy. While Lucy fed him strong tea (Dad was strongly opposed to boozing), we told him of our plans to emigrate to Australia. He mumbled about a brother of his in Canada, only two weeks away by ship and train in a place called British Columbia. He said he was earning ten pounds a week sawing down trees, and assured us that we could do just as well.

Charlie left after a while, and we sat around the kitchen debating what he had said. Someone suggested that "drunken men speak the truth," and with that bit of doubtful philosophy we changed our plans from Australia to Canada . . . Vancouver, B.C.

We went up to London the following Monday and got all the information available on British Columbia, and a few days later booked steerage passage on the Allen liner *Tunisian* to Halifax, with rail connections to Vancouver. The total fare was fifteen pounds (then seventy-five dollars). I still had thirty pounds of my racing prize money, which took care of my passage, outfitting, and at least five pounds over to land in Canada with. So I guess I was justified telling people in later years that I rowed my way from England to Canada.

Such a drastic parting of the ways was a bit of a wrench for all of us, but there seemed no hope of our making a decent living in England, so it had to be. There were tearful farewells at West Drayton and at the London station where we boarded the train for our port of embarkation, Liverpool. My one special chum of many years, Jimmy Ottrey, was there to bid us Godspeed also.

Many years later, Jimmy sent us a clipping of a BBC program titled "What's Wrong with English Rowing?" conducted by Jack Beresford, a famous amateur British oarsman, in which he said "We never should have let men like the Pococks get away from England."

But in the year of 1911, it seemed, only our loved ones were aware of our departure, and there was nothing but fond memories to keep us in the land of our birth.

2

Making Do on the Pacific Northwest Frontier

H AVING EMBARKED on the *Tunisian* at Liverpool, and found their way to the cramped steerage quarters well below the waterline, the Pocock brothers learned something known to all who had migrated to the Land of Promise in such accommodations. George put it succinctly, "Steerage is no bed of roses."

They occupied two of the six bunks in a minuscule and grubby cabin, three to a side with a narrow passage between. George, assigned to one of the uppermost, found minimal space between his thin mattress and the massive steel I-beams supporting the deck above. He also found, in due time, that these provided convenient runways for rats. Understandably, the brothers spent most of their time on deck enjoying the clean sea breeze.

On the first evening at sea, the main course of the steerage class dinner consisted of very greasy pork sausages. Most of the passengers, tired and hungry, "really tucked into them," George recalled.

He and Dick did not. Their training for competitive rowing paid off. They knew such fare was hard to digest and apt to produce biliousness. As a result of their prudence at the dinner table, they were among the very few steerage passengers who appeared at the breakfast table the next morning.

Their steward, an elderly man ending his sea career as he had begun it, at the bottom of the ladder, was a downcast and grouchy individual known to his passengers as "Old Merry and Bright." He unbent enough to confide to George and Dick that the sailing night menu was always the same, directed by the company as a means of creating mass *mal de mer* and an accompanying savings in the cost of rations to the steerage.

By the last evening of the eight-day crossing, most of lower deck passengers had recovered enough to stage a gala of sorts, although the final meal was no great improvement over the first. A dish which the stewards called Sea Pie was served. The Pocock brothers came to the conclusion that it consisted of all the leftovers from the galley, thriftily baked in doughy crust. George found it "decidedly unpalatable." Nevertheless, an impromptu concert was staged after dinner, with harmonica and accordion music, and a solo sung in a quavering voice by an emaciated individual who looked so sallow and sick that he had apparently been in his bunk ever since the first awful meal. When he had finished his feeble effort and the scattering of polite applause had faded into silence, a stentorian voice roared out, "Give him some Sea Pie!" That struck everyone as hilariously funny, and the celebration broke up amid gusts of semi-hysterical laughter.

In those days, Canada was still a part of the British Empire, and obtaining Canadian citizenship was a mere formality for the new arrivals. Nor was it surrounded by even a hint of pomp and circumstance. George recalled that the brief answering of questions and signing of papers was accomplished in a vastly overheated room at dockside, officiated over by a bored clerk in shirtsleeves with fancy garters to hold up his cuffs, and a button pinned to his shirt with the words "Kiss me Mabel."

The overland journey by train in "colonist cars" provided even fewer amenities than the steerage accommodations of the *Tunisian*. George remembered the long ride vividly in later years:

> We were now faced with a six-day railroad journey to Vancouver, B.C., and we were advised to buy a basket and fill it with enough food for the trip, which we did . . . bread, butter, cheese, sardines, doughnuts. We were all set. Three trains were waiting quite close to the dock. Dick and I got in the middle one, and quickly discovered that a colonist car was a step down from our cabin aboard ship. It wasn't much better than a boxcar, although it did have seats of sorts, and a long shelf which let down on chains parallel with the seats to provide a sleeping platform; no mattresses, just hard boards. No covers. Two laprobes we had brought along served for bedding; and of course, no undressing.
>
> To further mar the decor, a group of black-bearded Eastern Europeans of some kind were sitting across the aisle, all chewing tobacco, clearing their throats raucously, and spitting on the floor. Dick told them to cease and desist, but they obviously didn't understand English. When he stood up to his full height and shook his fist at them, however, they stopped immediately.
>
> The colonist train, we found, was sidetracked for all other rail traffic. Immigrants, it

was apparent, had no priority, either afloat or ashore. It seemed that we spent as much time on sidings to make way for freight trains, express trains, cattle trains, and everything else on flanged wheels as we did moving. There were also long halts at stations to take on coal and water, and to allow the colonists to restock their food supplies. We still had plenty to eat, although the bread was getting noticeably stale. During these stops I reached the conclusion that Canadian towns were very religious. We could hear church bells tolling at every one of them . . . until at one stop we walked up to the locomotive and discovered that, unlike English trains, the ones in Canada were equipped with bells as well as whistles.

But I soon found that petty dishonesty and cruelty were not limited geographically. An example was provided by a number of small-time crooks who called themselves "news vendors." They went through the cars with large baskets of candy bars, fruit, cigarettes, and such. If they were offered currency, they substituted nickels for quarters in making change. Canadian nickels were about the same size as quarters, and most of the immigrants couldn't tell the difference. I thought this robbing of poor foreigners, most of whom possessed barely enough to survive in their new world, was a classic example of man's inhumanity to man.

The journey from England to the West Coast of Canada took two weeks. The young immigrants arrived tired, dirty, and nearly broke:

We finally arrived in Vancouver on March 23, 1911, having sailed from Liverpool March 9. We hadn't had a bath or a shave in two weeks, and we had slept in our clothes amid the soot and grime of the colonist car. We were pretty rough looking characters. We walked up Granville Street and entered a building with a "rooms for rent" sign at the entrance, and were informed the cost would be $16 a week. We asked what time meals were served. The price didn't include meals! In those days you could rent a fairly respectable hotel room for a dollar a night or less, so we quickly departed. It was obvious the proprietor viewed us as undesirables and had quoted the outrageous rate to discourage us.

We left Granville Street and walked a block over to Burrard Street, which was lined with private homes. We soon found one with a "for rent" sign and were given a neat, clean room for two dollars a week. We even had baths, and I can still remember how wonderful it felt to be clean again. Looking reasonably respectable, we strolled the streets in wonder at this big city; big anyway in comparison to the rural Thames River villages we were accustomed to. Vancouver boosters were boasting a population of fifty thousand then, but I think that took in at least a twelve-mile radius. Today it is a truly beautiful metropolitan city and the largest port in Canada.

We stopped at a cafe for supper and gorged ourselves on soup, delicious fresh grilled salmon, vegetables, dessert, and coffee. It was truly a feast after what we had been existing on from the *Tunisian*'s steerage class galley and the basket of provisions on the colonist train. The check came to 25¢ apiece.

Although surrounded by the most magnificent scenery . . . . expanses of salt water,

timbered hills, and snow-capped mountains, Vancouver seemed somehow raw and unfinished to us, used as we were to the lovingly tended greens and mellow, centuries-old
castles and buildings of Eton and Westminister. But it was apparent that this was an
up-and-coming city, with a great deal of building activity. The people were different,
too, from the relaxed folk we had known in the quiet villages along the gently flowing
Thames. Here, the people on the streets moved fast and seemed tense . . . as though
they all had great projects in mind and no time to waste.

The principal industrial activity in Vancouver was the milling of lumber. The mills
were all located on the waterfront, which stretched for miles below the city. The sound
of whirring saws and the pleasant scent of freshly sawn Douglas fir and western red
cedar permeated the air. Huge booms of logs rested in the water at every mill, waiting
to be hauled ashore and cut into finished lumber.

Aside from the mills, we saw no other manufacturing plants, except a few very small
ones which could not have employed more than a few workers. But this was more than
made up for by the amazing number of real estate offices. We concluded that the selling
of land was the second biggest industry in Vancouver.

The somewhat homesick young Britishers were cheered considerably when they
located a scientific instrument and camera shop operated by a boyhood friend, Fred
Goertz. Fred was the son of a respected Windsor furniture dealer and repairman, who
was frequently called upon for skilled work at Windsor Castle. Young Goertz made
them feel a bit more welcome to this big and alien city.

The depleted state of their finances, however, permitted little time for sightseeing
or socializing. The hunt for work couldn't be delayed. There was no demand on the
Vancouver labor market for builders of racing shells, however skilled, so despite their
years of painstaking apprenticeship, George and Dick were unskilled labor as far as
British Columbia employers were concerned.

There were numerous employment offices where, for a fee in advance, men could
"buy" a job. Dick counted out the required sum from his rapidly diminishing store
of coins, and was assigned to work as a "rough carpenter" at Coquitlam, about fifteen
miles east of Vancouver. British Columbia government officials had been convinced
that agricultural work would have a therapeutic effect on inmates of the provincial
insane asylum, and Dick was to help build the psychiatric farm. Arriving in Coquitlam
by train, he was met at the station by a man who informed him he was in charge of
the entire project and, in fact, owned the town and everything else for miles around.

Dick concluded that former residents of the mental hospital had been assigned to
assist in the building of their new home, as indeed they had. Some of them added
bizarre touches to Dick's unfamiliar job. One had a habit of sneaking up behind
workers as they waited to load up at a concrete mixer and shoving them into their
wheelbarrows. He was fleet of foot, and the enraged victims were never able to catch

him. Another who made Dick a bit nervous was an elderly Chinese man who wandered around the construction site with a big stack of toilet paper, which he continually counted, apparently under the impression that it was money.

Nor did Dick exactly distinguish himself. His first assignment was to hang a door, which was something he had never done before. He installed it upside-down and backward, so it swung in the wrong direction. Then he placed the handle at a convenient height for his six-foot-five-inch reach. The little Chinese gentleman with the fortune in toilet paper couldn't reach it. Finally Dick screwed on the lock, forgetting to first make a hole for the key. He borrowed a brace and bit and tried to guess where to bore the hole. He miscalculated, hit the metal, and broke the bit. His only major accomplishment on that job was the saving of a fellow worker who jumped into an icy river after work and immediately began to drown. Dick went in after him and dragged him out, which was something he *did* have experience in. According to George, his brother already had three or four rescues to his credit in England.

George had in the meantime secured a job of sorts at the Vancouver Rowing Club on Coal Harbor. He reported for duty on April 1, eight days after their arrival on the colonist train. He recalled his first water-oriented job in North America in later years:

> The wages were $40.00 a month, or $1.30 a day. My duties were to repair boats (which they certainly needed) and to assist the oarsman in and out of them. The boats were in frightful shape. The very first four-oared shell that went out, the crew took one stroke, the blades went down deep, and they almost tipped over. I called them back, found a piece of 2 × 4 lumber, and adjusted their riggers to put more pitch in the rowlocks. They tried again, with much better results, and waved to me, as much as to say "He knows his job."
>
> Although the work itself was congenial, I only stayed about a month, sleeping in one of the sheds and eating poorly since there were no cooking facilities. I felt I had to earn more money, so I took a job in a logging camp away up in the interior of British Columbia. It entailed a long journey by train and a thirty-mile hike into the camp itself.

George's tribulations at the remote logging camp included the accidental breaking of a cross-cut saw, for which he was docked more than two days' pay, but the last straw was his assignment to supply firewood and water to the steam dockey engine. The engine had just been moved far up a hillside, too far from the river for its suction pipe to reach. George was supposed to struggle up and down the steep hill filling two fifty-two-gallon barrels from tin pails, then saw wood like mad for the boiler fire. When the engineer turned the valve to fill his boiler, the barrels would suck dry and George would drop his saw, grab the pails, and head for the river again. Realizing he was killing himself, he quit after a month at the camp and returned to Vancouver,

The Vancouver Rowing Club, early 1900s (photo courtesy of Jack Carver)

where he found a job stacking lumber at a sawmill and rented a room above a Chinese restaurant.

He later learned that, upon his departure, two husky men were assigned to the job he had held. "That, made me feel better," he said. "I had never considered myself a weakling, and I was beginning to wonder if that was the usual output expected of a man working in British Columbia."

He then got a better-paying job at the Vancouver Shipyard, in the course of which he suffered a serious injury to his right hand, which resulted in the loss of two fingers.

By the time he had recovered, winter had set in, the logging camps were mostly shut down, and jobs were hard to find. He and his brother rejoined forces, working as laborers on the remodeling of a downtown Vancouver building.

The injury to his hand and lack of money put a final end to George's dream of returning home in 1912, his year for a try at the Doggett's Coat and Badge. Another sculler, whom he had beaten in the past, took home the livery and badge that year.

But things were taking a turn for the better nonetheless. Early in 1912 the Pocock brothers were able to return to the craft for which they had been trained, and which they loved. True, the conditions under which they would work were primitive, but they would be building racing shells again, and that was enough for them at the moment. They were beginning to put down roots in the new world as their ties to the old were receding into pleasant memories. From now on they would be far too busy to be homesick. As George recalled later:

> A recent arrival in Canada, a Mr. Hudson, who had rowed at Cambridge, joined the Vancouver Rowing Club at about this time. He had evidently heard of our boatbuilding abilities and our sculling achievements. We were asked to attend a meeting of the club committee one Saturday evening. After we had answered many questions, they were apparently satisfied that we knew our trade. We were told they would give us an initial order for two singles if we were willing to meet their conditions. They would pay us $200 for the two boats.
>
> The club had a very old shed floating on logs nearby, which they would let us have for $100 for use as a workshop and residence. It was a good deal for them, since the shed was something of an eyesore and they would probably have had to pay to have it demolished. They made it clear that we couldn't leave it where it was, but would have to move it out into Coal Harbor, where the members wouldn't have to look at it.
>
> Still, it was our chance to get back into the boatbuilding business, and our only qualms lay in the fact that we didn't have the required $100 purchase price. I solved that by heading up town to a loan office, where I showed the $200 boat order as collateral and got a thirty-day loan of $100, signing a note to repay $110 at the end of the month. We had a little money saved, but that would be needed for building material and living expenses. And since we had to move the floathouse offshore, that meant buying anchors and chain.

The ancient two-story "float," the original headquarters of the Vancouver Rowing Club, would have provided more qualms than one to less optimistic entrepreneurs than the young Pocock brothers (Dick had just turned twenty-three; George was barely twenty-one). In its "glory days" as a clubhouse, its upper floor had been euphemistically called "the caretaker's living quarters." The lower floor had been used to store the club's small fleet of boats: singles, doubles, and fours. It wasn't long enough to hold a regular eight-oared shell.

"The Float": first workshop of George and Dick Pocock in Coal Harbor, Vancouver, B.C., 1911

The "living quarters" consisted of a sleeping room and a primitive cooking area containing an ancient and rusty wood stove. Of course there was neither electricity nor running water. The brothers hauled drinking water from a public fountain in nearby Stanley Park, admired the marine view from their bedroom window, took baths by diving through it into the harbor, and George, ever the philosopher, observed that "the spirit of man is his strength and our spirits were not broken."

The work of building a fragile and delicately tuned racing shell has been aptly likened to the making of a fine violin, and it would have been hard to find a less likely place for such precise and painstaking tasks than the lower floor of the old floathouse. Twice each day, the tide not only came into Coal Harbor, it came into the Pococks' workshop.

"We found that, at low tide, our building's float logs would rest in the mud of the harbor bottom," George recalled. "Their years of immersion had left them water-logged, and the weight prevented their floating up as the tide came in. The water would rise in the shop while we took refuge on the steps to the room above and tried to estimate when the next act of the daily drama would occur. Eventually, with a swish and a roar, the logs would break the mud's hold, and up would come the building, like a surfacing submarine, with the water rushing out the doors at each end. Then we could start working again   until the next change of the tide.

"One very low tide, one of the logs remained stuck and remained behind when the rest of the lash-up made its dramatic rise from the deep. After a while it broke loose and came up with a rush and a crash. It was hard on our nerves and, worse, it caused the building to float with a definite list to starboard."

Undaunted, the brothers made allowances for the lopsided aspect of their floating workshop in the building of the forty-foot stocks, or base, upon which they would build the four-oared shells. This structure was built of two prime cedar 2 × 12 planks, giving full-length support to the shells under construction and protecting them from the distortion which would otherwise have resulted from the unpredictable gyrations of the workshop. (In 1972, George recalled that these splendid cedar planks cost them two dollars each, noting that "if you could find them today, they would cost at least twenty times as much.")

But their adventures afloat on Coal Harbor were not over. Wind as well as tide was a hazard to the Pocock's floating establishment, as George recalled in his memoirs:

On waking we would always check our position through the bedroom window. One morning we looked out and saw the Canadian Pacific Steamship dock coming into sight, and we were still moving. A blow during the night had dragged the anchors and we were sailing through the harbor at a fine clip. Literally sailing. The size of the building afforded a frightful resistance to the wind, just like a giant squaresail.

We hurriedly dressed and went outside. A motorboat soon hove into sight and we frantically waved at the pilot. He drew alongside, but doubted that he had enough power to tow us back against the wind. He managed it, however, and we gave him a two dollar reward; it was a lot of money, but we agreed he deserved it.

The old adage that "it's an ill wind that blows no good" was certainly true in this case. At the spot where he left us, we soon discovered that the bottom was smooth and hard. The logs no longer stuck in the mud at low tides, allowing us to work regardless of the tide. We quickly finished two singles for the club (and one for ourselves), and rowed the club boats over for inspection and payment. The club captain wanted to "see them in action," so Dick and I rowed a couple of laps in front of the club. The captain seemed impressed, and we got our $200; enough to pay off our loan in full and to add a few dollars to the company treasury.

Word was by then spreading through the very limited but highly enthusiastic British Columbia rowing fraternity that professionally built racing and practice shells were actually obtainable within the province. There was a mild celebration aboard the "float" when an order came in from the inland town of Kelowna, where some former British oarsmen were forming a club on Okanagan Lake, for three practice fours for $1,000. Racing shells and lapstrake practice boats traditionally were planked with Spanish cedar, the same material from which old-fashioned cigar boxes were made. George finally located a hardwood dealer in San Francisco, who sent a load of the Mexican-produced wood to Vancouver by ship. By the time they had manhandled the shipment from the dock, they had a backlog of new orders: two fours for the James Bay Athletic Club of Victoria, and one for the Prince Rupert Rowing Club, all lapstrake practice boats.

The three craft for Kelowna were duly shipped via Canadian Pacific Railway Express, but one of them was seriously damaged in transit. The express company sent George to Kelowna by rail to make repairs, and he found his three-day visit there a pleasant experience.

"I spent my time in Kelowna completing the repairs and going out rowing every evening with different members of the club, and really had a grand time. I am sure, too, the members enjoyed my coaching them in the style of the Thames watermen, which stresses the maximum speed with the minimum of effort. Getting back to the 'float' as we called our building on logs in Coal Harbor, I had plenty to tell Dick."

A few days later, as they were hard at work on their latest order for practice boats, the Pocock brothers gazed out the window at a weird and wonderful sight.

The wind was brisk, the water was rough, and a well-dressed man was trying hard, but with a total lack of skill, to row a skiff to their floating workshop. He frequently "caught a crab" slashing the water with a mis-turned oar, and seemd to lose at least a foot for every two feet of headway he made toward them. He was also making a lot of leeway, frequently glancing over his shoulder hopefully.

When the stranger finally made it to within hailing distance, the brothers shouted against the wind, asking if he wanted to come aboard. He nodded his head emphatically and they got their long-handled boathook, harpooned his skiff, and dragged it alongside.

Damp and windblown, but recovering rapidly from his ordeal, the stranger intro-

Hiram Conibear, 1914

duced himself: "My name is Hiram Conibear. I am the rowing coach at the University of Washington in Seattle."

The Pocock brothers glanced at each other in some disbelief. His performance in the rowboat had been anything but professional. In fact, it had been so bad that George recalled, "we actually thought he was under the influence of liquor."

Abandoning their belief that drunks always tell the truth, which had prompted their migration to Canada, George politely worked himself around to a position where he could unobtrusively sniff their visitor's breath. There wasn't a trace of alcohol on it, so the brothers came to the wondering conclusion that this clumsiest of oarsmen was, indeed, the rowing coach at the University of Washington.

Hiram Conibear was to become a legendary figure, but his championship University of Washington crew program was only a hopeful gleam in his eye when the Pocock brothers first met him. When his eight-oared, Pocock-built shells began sweeping to victory after victory, Seattle newspapers were inspired to dwell on the marvels of something they called "the Conibear Stroke."

Years afterward, with the restrained humor that was one of his hallmarks, George observed dryly, "On that stormy day in 1912, ours were the only eyes in this area to gaze in wonder upon the Conibear Stroke."

3

Building Shells in the Tokyo Tea Room

THE POCOCKS didn't know it, but the erratic arrival of Hiram Conibear in his borrowed skiff marked another major turning point in their lives. Conibear had heard of their boatbuilding and rowing skills, he had seen and admired the four-oared shells they had built for the Vancouver Rowing Club, and he had come to the conclusion that they were just what he needed to get the eight-year-old rowing program at the University of Washington properly off the ground. And what he wanted, he usually got. One way or another.

With introductions completed, the brothers ushered him into their shop, where he picked up a flat piece of spruce, seated himself on a stool, and sketched the rowing paradise upon which he planned to launch his program . . . Lake Union, where the college boathouse was located, the proposed ship canal that would link Lake Union with much larger Lake Washington, and the broad sweep of the university campus overlooking and bordering on the lakes. It looked impressive.

The Pocock brothers were even more impressed when Conibear told them he would need twelve eight-oared shells for starters. He wanted them to move to Seattle, where space would be provided for their shop on campus. Somewhat dazed, they agreed to come to Seattle to look things over and make up their minds. George recalled, "We practically bowed him back into his boat, and watched him struggle away toward shore, muttering to ourselves, 'Rowing coach at the University of Washington. Oh my, oh my!' "

Their feeling that there was something a bit improbable about their visitor was borne out by the facts. Conibear *was* the rowing coach at the University of Washington,

34

Washington's first crew was a four without coxswain, pictured here in 1903. Left to right: Fred McElmon, Clint Lantz, Dan Pullen, Carl Van Kuran

and he did *need* a dozen shells, but at the moment he didn't have a dime toward paying for them. Nor did he explain that the space he had reserved for them on campus consisted of a tottery structure erected in a single day to serve as a Japanese tea room. Connie hadn't lied to them, but he hadn't wasted time on a lot of nitpicking details either.

Hiram Conibear had had a varied career in sports. A one-time professional bicycle racer, he had also been a team trainer in big league baseball, and had been the trainer of the track team at the University of Chicago. At the University of Washington he had been a sort of athletic man-of-all-work, pinch-hitting wherever he might be needed. When it was decided in 1904 to add rowing to the major sports program, he

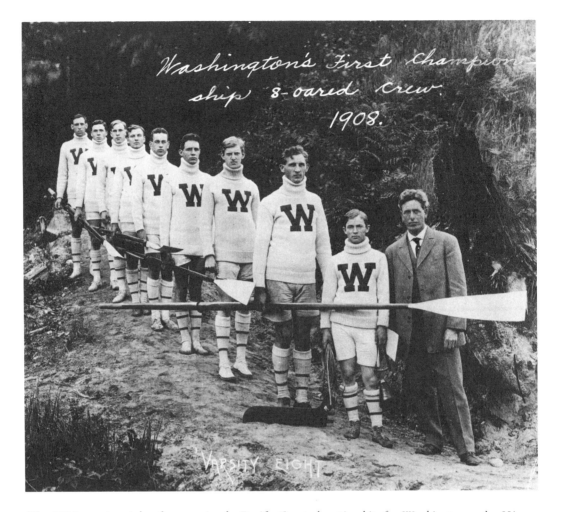

The 1908 varsity eight, first to win the Pacific Coast championship for Washington under Hiram Conibear. The crew included Arthur Aarr, Brous Beck, Homer Kirby, Bart Lovejoy, Doak Lowry, F. L. O'Brien, Arthur O'Neal, Ev Thomsen, and Hart Willis.

was named head coach of a sport in which he had not an iota of experience. The truest thing of all was that he needed the Pocock brothers.

Once embarked on his new profession, Conibear gave it everything he had. He was paid a small salary by the Associated Student Body, but nothing from university funds. Nor were any funds budgeted to organize and operate his department. He set out to collect what he termed "voluntary funds," a slow process at first, but as time went by and his crews brought honor and prestige to the university and the Pacific Northwest, a lot of alumni and Seattle businessmen found it was difficult indeed to say no to Conibear's fund drives.

He was equally devoted to the science of rowing. He even borrowed a human

THE OLD VARSITY BOAT CLUB

The old Alaska-Yukon-Pacific Exposition Coast Guard station in use as first University of Washington crewhouse

skeleton from a university laboratory and spent painstaking hours placing it in various positions he conceived to be involved in a proper oarsman's stroke, making detailed graphs of the results.

On July 12, 1912, the Pocock brothers boarded the Canadian Pacific day steamer for Seattle for a pleasant voyage of several hours through some of the world's most beautiful scenery. They spent the night at a no-frills downtown hotel and took a streetcar to the university campus. Conibear met them at the car stop on Brooklyn Avenue, and the morning was spent in touring the campus.

The British-born Pococks were not favorably impressed. They had expected something like the ivied halls and manicured lawns of Eton or Cambridge. Instead they saw only three or four permanent buildings, the rest flimsy structures with the impermanent look of stage sets. George's first impression of Washington's most prestigious institution of higher education was of "a sad looking place."

The old Tokyo Tea Room, used by George and Dick Pocock for shell-building from 1912 to 1916

Conibear explained that the campus had been the site, three years earlier, of the Alaska-Yukon-Pacific Exposition, a forerunner of Seattle's 1962 World Fair. The fast-growing university had taken over many of the temporary buildings, which were mostly of thin framework and plaster construction. And the plaster was falling off most of them. The "shell house" on Lake Union proved to be an abandoned Coast Guard station, also lightly built as a temporary structure for the run of the fair.

The structure Conibear had promised to fit out for shell building was even flimsier. "This building, the Tokyo Tea Room, was put up in 24 hours by volunteer Japanese carpenters, and it looked like it," George wrote. "It was poorly lighted, and we told him so, but he cheerfully waved that criticism aside. Not to worry, he assured us. He would have that taken care of if we decided to accept his offer. We also noticed that the building would actually shake and tremble as we walked around in it, but we told ourselves that at least it was on solid ground."

Promising to think it over, the brothers returned to their hotel. Next morning, for a dollar each, they boarded a special sightseeing streetcar for what was advertised as a "Trip de Luxe." The first stop after leaving the totem pole in Pioneer Square was a vast excavation on Second Avenue, which the barker proclaimed to be "the future site of the forty-two-story L. C. Smith Building, the tallest building west of the Mississippi." He pointed out other structural wonders of 1912 Seattle: the Hoge Building, "a world's record in steel construction, ten stories in ten days," and the New Washington Hotel, built at the location of a steep hill that had once blocked the city's expansion to the north. The hill had been washed into Puget Sound by the hydraulic methods used by the Klondike miners of the Alaska gold rush.

The sightseeing trolley carried them out for another walking tour of the university campus, where the barker dramatically announced that Mount Rainier, "the tallest peak in the United States," was to be seen in all its glory to the south, "the second time this year that it has been visible to human eyes." George gazed up at the perpetual snow and ice of the great peak and had to concede there was nothing to match that in England. He certainly didn't imagine that, fifteen years later, he would stand at the summit of that 14,408-foot volcanic giant and look down to where it had all begun on a bright July day in 1912. Although the water was his first love, he often took inland holidays, climbing the mountains and exploring the vast wilderness areas of the Northwest country that became his home.

After a launch trip across Lake Washington and another streetcar back to Pioneer Square, the Pococks caught the night boat back to Vancouver, both quiet and deep in thought. Their conservative English upbringing made the heady atmosphere of booming Seattle a bit unreal to them.

"One of our thoughts," according to George, "was what kind of meat do those people in Seattle feed on?" It was obvious that they were dreaming grand dreams, and a lot of those dreams were coming true. Maybe Hiram Conibear's grand dream of a world class crew program at the University of Washington would come true also. After all, they rationalized, "if they already had a full-fledged rowing department they wouldn't have wanted us."

The next day George posted a letter to Conibear, telling him they would come to Seattle and build his twelve eight-oared shells. The brothers had kept close contact with the family back in England, and were aware that their father was more or less footloose at the moment. They invited him to come to America to help them build Conibear's fleet. Late in July, they received word that he was coming, and bringing sisters Lucy and Kath with him. He expected to arrive in Vancouver on October 10. George and Dick spent the intervening months finishing up a number of singles, doubles, and fours for Canadian rowing clubs. As the time of family reunion drew near, they rented a room near the harbor for their sisters. Soon they would leave for Seattle and that twelve-shell job.

With Aaron and the girls already en route to Vancouver, the brothers received a letter from Conibear which blew their plans and hopes right out of the water. The

Climbing Mount Rainier with Clyde Adams, 1927

Sir Thomas Lipton (third from left), tea tycoon and America's Cup racing yacht owner, visits the University of Washington crewhouse in 1913. Hiram Conibear, in derby, center; George Pocock, far right

ever-optimistic coach had been able to raise only enough money for *one* shell—not the twelve they had been counting on.

Their father, who was used to coping with reverses, only smiled and said, "You must remember that Mr. Conibear is an American."

Many years later, an American citizen and very proud of it, George remembered with sorrow his father's comment, which he knew reflected an opinion of American character widely held in other lands. "We who are Americans," he wrote, "know that there are only a few of that sort in the United States, and it behooves every American to watch his step or, in this case, his tongue." It was typical of George that he viewed such defense of America's honor as a very personal responsibility, as deeply imbedded in his character as his religious convictions.

He was also a gentle man, and a forgiving one. "Connie can be excused," he wrote, "because he was so deeply committed to the excellence of rowing at the University of Washington, and was so anxious to get us down to Seattle."

Making the best of a disappointing situation, the Pococks decided that Dick and Aaron would go to Seattle to build the single eight-oared shell, while George would continue to operate the float in Coal Harbor.

The university eight—the first of a great fleet of legendary Pocock-built racing shells—was duly completed and christened *Rodgers* in honor of the Seattle candy manufacturer whose $200 donation had been the most generous one made to Conibear's building fund.

No sooner had Dick and Aaron returned to Vancouver than Conibear wrote again. Stanford University had received glowing reports of Washington's new shell, and wanted one just like it. This time George and his father went to Seattle, along with Lucy and Kath. Conibear, who was anxious to do all he could to make up for the fiasco of the eleven phantom shells, saw that the two girls were provided with modestly paid jobs. Arthur E. Campbell, a crew member who was also the first manager of the crew quarters, remembers hiring them to work in the kitchen. Lucy was chief cook for the crew training table, and Kath was her assistant.

When the men returned to Vancouver they found that orders had come in for more boats than the floating shop could handle. Space was provided for building stocks in the new Vancouver Rowing Club building. Dick and Aaron worked there on larger craft—a coaching gig and racing fours—while George built singles and doubles on the old float.

When the backlog of work in Vancouver was cleaned up, Aaron admitted that he was homesick for England and the Thames, and was going to return. The brothers would not see him again for more than twenty years. Aaron went back by way of Seattle for his farewells to his daughters, and to accompany the University of Washington crew on its first trip to the famed Intercollegiate Regatta at Poughkeepsie, New York, in June 1913.

The Pococks had spent much time with Conibear, persuading him to modify the "over-actioned" stroke he had developed from his theoretical studies of the borrowed skeleton. The "Conibear Stroke" of 1913 owed much to the Pocock-inspired overtones of the traditional Thames Waterman Stroke, with its emphasis on achieving maximum speed with minimum fuss and effort.[1]

1. The "Conibear Stroke" became almost a household word in the early glory days of Washington crew racing, but nobody seemed to know exactly what it was, not even Conibear himself. When pressed, his only definition of it was "it's the stroke that gets you there." One veteran crewman of the Conibear era said it was impossible to describe because it "changed every year."

Washington's 1913 crew, the first to qualify for the Poughkeepsie Regatta, wear stylish traveling uniforms on the trip to New York. Back row, from left: Ed Leader, Ed Taylor, Archie Campbell, Wilson Lee, Clarke Will, Heine Zimmerman; middle: Will Hutton, Max Walske, George Hutton; front: Elmer Leader, Russell Callow, A. G. Campbell, Paul Hammer (photo courtesy of Sandra Plush).

Whatever the Conibear-(Pocock) Stroke of 1913 was, it worked pretty well. Washington was acclaimed Pacific Coast champion when it outraced both California and Stanford. The resulting enthusiasm was such that Conibear had little difficulty in extracting a $4,000 gift from Mr. Frye of the Frye Packing Company, to finance the trip to Poughkeepsie where the national championship would be decided.

Washington's rookie oarsmen came in third, behind the winner, Syracuse, and runner-up Cornell, but it was a neck-and-neck finish with less than half a shell-length separating the three leaders. Pennsylvania and Wisconsin were fourth and fifth respectively

This was hailed as a victory in Seattle, and it was certainly no mean achievement for a crew with little previous experience and no rowing tradition behind it. Local

University of Washington freshman women's crew, ca. 1915

Practicing on Lake Union, ca. 1914 (photo courtesy of the Historical Society of Seattle and King County)

University of Washington varsity crew, 1915. From left to right: Paul Hammer, Heine Zimmerman,
Clyde Brokaw, Russell "Rusty" Callow, Adolph "Short" Harr, Harold Waller, Paul McConihe,
Ward Kumm, Art "Stub" Ward (photo courtesy of Frank S. Evans). This photo was declared "indecent"
by the editor of the Tyee, *the UW yearbook. It was censored and replaced with the more modest picture*
on the right (photo courtesy of Sandra Plush).

businessmen and alumni throughout the state who had turned cold shoulders to Conibear's previous fund-raising efforts now began to rally around him, pledging funds to
buy him two new eights. The Pocock brothers agreed to build them for $500 each,
and returned to the Tokyo Tea Room in October 1913. By the time the two new
shells, *Seattle Spirit I* and *Seattle Spirit II,* were finished, the indefatigable Conibear
had sold the university on an effort to restore interest in the moribund women's rowing
program,[2] and the brothers received orders for two eight-oared "co-ed" barges and

2. In those early years, women's rowing was a part of the program, although actual racing was
considered far too strenuous for what was then referred to as the "weaker sex." Women were judged
on style rather than speed, and upon the chicness of their uniforms, which they were required to
design and make themselves. Understandably, interest in it soon died. Women's rowing was eliminated
in 1917, then reinstituted in the 1960s as an intramural sport. It is now a full-fledged intercollegiate
varsity sport.

two barge fours. Soon other orders came in, from the Portland Rowing Club for two barge fours, and from Coeur d'Alene, Idaho, for three shells.

By the end of 1913, the Pocock brothers had decided to make Seattle their home. They turned over the Coal Harbor float to an ancient waterfront character named

Dave Keeley to sell for them. He sold it for sixty dollars, and was given half the price as his commission. It was a major windfall for the old timer, whom George remembered fondly for having taken him to visit Robert Louis Stevenson's famous schooner *Casco*, which was moored in Vancouver harbor. The author and his wife weren't aboard, but the great man's desk and chair were, and George Pocock, ever the lover of great literature, imagined him at work on *Treasure Island* or *Dr. Jekyll and Mr. Hyde.*

The artisan and craftsman in the young Englishman was not to be denied either. "What I particularly noticed," he wrote in later years, "was the steering wheel shaft connected to the rudder. It had a diamond thread so that the pilot did not have to let go of the wheel to haul on different spokes, but just pumped the wheel to work the rudder. A flip of a cog and it would act the opposite way, similar to a Yankee screwdriver."

With affairs disposed of in Vancouver, the Pocock brothers and sisters established their first real home in the New World. They rented a modest house on Fifteenth Avenue N.E., in the University District of Seattle. The rent was eleven dollars a month (they could have bought the house outright for $1,200), and they went on a shopping spree with the Sears Roebuck catalog, selecting all their household furnishings from its pages. Dick and George were earning enough to pay the rent and household expenses. Lucy, a rowing champion in her own right in England, had been promoted by Conibear to coach of the women's crews. When the season ended, she put her cooking skills to work in the kitchen of a University Way restaurant, and sometimes made extra money as coach at the old Moore Hotel swimming pool in downtown Seattle. Kath was taking a secretarial course at a local business college. They lived modestly but, as George recalled, "we were a very happy foursome."

The next three years passed with relative tranquillity for the Pacific Northwest, Seattle, and the Pococks, although Europe was aflame with the most destructive war the world had yet seen. But by 1916, battle flags were also flying at the University of Washington. Dr. Henry Suzzallo had been appointed president of the university in 1915. A distinguished scholar and administrator possessed of a dominating personality, he was determined to establish the University of Washington as one of the nation's great institutions of higher learning. In the decade he held his post, he went far toward achieving that goal, gaining national prominence in the process.

In the meantime, Suzzallo toppled a number of campus idols, among them the legendary football coach, Gilmour ("Gloomy Gil") Dobie, and Hiram Conibear.

Dobie had come from North Dakota Agricultural College in 1908. He revolutionized and refined football from the primitive power plays of the past, his tricky "bunk" plays becoming as famous as the "Conibear Stroke." From the time of his arrival until 1916, no Washington team ever lost a game. That year a spate of injuries had weakened the team, and the star tackle, Bill Grimm, was suspended for alleged "examination irregularities" just prior to the final crucial game with California. Suzzallo backed the suspension and the rest of the team went on a two-day protest strike. Feelings were at a high pitch on November 20, and a screaming crowd of nearly ten thousand, the largest ever assembled at University Field, nearly went crazy when the underdog Washington team beat mighty California 14 to 7.

The victory cost Dobie his job. In demand all over the nation, he had resigned the previous year, probably aware of Suzzallo's hostility toward him and the domination of athletics over scholastic education on the campus. He had been persuaded to return after a conference in which it had seemed Suzzallo had approved of his doing so. Now his fame and popularity had exceeded the president's. He was fired.

Conibear was also caught in the line of fire of Suzzallo's battle to end the domination of athletic coaches, and to place education above sports in importance.

Connie, George Pocock conceded, had an unfortunate tendency to meddle in campus affairs. His crews, like Dobie's football teams, were growing powers in Pacific Coast athletics, and the impulsive and freewheeling crew coach had occasional brainstorms which brought embarrassment to the university. One occurred in 1912, but it was so spectacular that it was still a matter of humorous comment years later. George had this recollection of the event:

There were to be two races that year, one between the California and Washington varsity eights; the other between the two JV crews. It was to be rowed over a three-mile course on Lake Washington, and Connie got the bright idea of speeding up the action. The varsity crews were lined up at one end of the course; the JV's at the other. As soon as the varsity race ended, the umpire would turn his launch around and start the other race going in the opposite direction.

Those were the days when motor launches were allowed to follow the races, and sizable fleets of them had gathered at both ends of the course, crowded with fans ready to cheer on their favorites. Connie himself was the umpire and starter, but for some reason there was a long delay in starting the first race. Three miles away, the spectators grew restless, and the crews muttered wrathfully as the cold breeze cooled them and their muscles cramped. Finally they persuaded a lesser official, in charge at that end of the course, to give them the starting signal.

As ill fortune would have it, the crew at the other end started off full-bore at about the same time and, heaven forbid, the racing crews and the following launches met halfway, and to describe the awful mix-up would require a better pen than mine . . . crews trying to dodge each other, launches in near collisions, the water boiling, oarsmen catching crabs, and Connie in the bow of the only official launch bashing his megaphone over the bow of his launch in utter disbelief of what he was seeing. If an old-fashioned Keystone comedy had been planned that way it couldn't have been funnier.

Conibear's second unfortunate innovation also took place on Lake Washington, or rather along its shoreline. George also recalled that one vividly after a lapse of half a century:

There was a stretch along the shore from Sand Point where a railroad track almost paralleled the lake for six miles. Connie's idea was to charter a train, sell tickets to passengers, and keep it moving along the shoreline while five intramural crew races were staged; a one-mile singles race, then a one-mile doubles race, followed by a one-mile pair-oared race and, finally, a two-mile race between eight-oared shells.

The train idea was a popular and financial success, but Connie's overenthusiastic efforts to please its paying passengers resulted in something of a disaster. He had noticed that shoreside trees sometimes blocked the view from the railroad tracks. Among the men turning out for crew in those days were many who earned the money for their college expenses by working as part-time loggers in the Pacific Northwest forests. He recruited a party of these skilled treecutters, took them to the lakeshore, and put them to work with axes and cross-cut saws. They made quick work of the offending trees and cleared the view nicely, but Connie had overlooked the fact that his demolition squad was operating on private property. When the owners found their trees felled, they had their attorneys contact the University with threats of both criminal and civil law suits. How the University finally settled with them I do not know, but I do know it didn't increase Connie's popularity in the front office.

Although Conibear is usually remembered for his flamboyant exploits, he also showed a genuine concern for the young athletes he trained. When sixteen-year-old H. W. McCurdy turned out for the freshman crew in 1916, his mother wrote Conibear, expressing concern for her boy's health. Years later, at the time of his mother's death, McCurdy found the following letter:

My Dear Mrs. McCurdy;—

Yours of the 7th inst at hand some few days ago and I have watched your boy very carefully since and I am satisfied that he is receiving just the kind of work and discipline that he needs. He is quite tired some times no doubt but I am sure that the work will not hurt him if he does the other things that we ask and expect him to do. We want him to eat at meal times only. We want him to be in bed every night and asleep at 10:30 each night. Then when he is in the boat and working we expect him to develop skill and to learn to know himself and thus be able to distribute his strength in the hour he is in the boat.

I have not as yet had a talk with the boy personally but I shall in a few days and then we shall understand one another much better.

I am indeed pleased to hear from you and to know that there are some parents that do watch their boys when they are in the University and do not send them to college simply to get rid of the work and worry of looking after them. You can rest assured that there is nothing that I am more interested in than in the physical development of the boy and of doing all I can to make more out of the boy than just an athlete.

Hoping that you will find time sometime when you are in the city to come out and see the crew men work out and to learn something of the spirit that is in crew men.

Sincerely yours
H. P. Conibear

Not only was Conibear kind enough to allay a mother's anxiety—he also showed supreme tact in not even hinting to McCurdy that the correspondence had taken place.

When Suzzallo fired Conibear, Rusty Callow, who pulled stroke oar on the varsity crew and was president of the Associated Student Body, intervened on the coach's behalf. Suzzallo finally agreed to let Conibear stay if he would promise to keep his nose out of campus politics and spend six months in the East learning how to row a boat.

Connie performed his penance and returned to Seattle in the fall of 1916 to find his backyard orchard heavy with fruit. That evening he had dinner with Arthur Campbell and his wife.[3] The next day he fell from a tree while picking plums and was killed.

The colorful pioneer era of collegiate rowing at the University of Washington died with Hiram Conibear on that October day.

George and Dick Pocock mourned the passing of this intense, mercurial man who had, in his own sometimes peculiar way, been a good friend to them. It was difficult to envision collegiate rowing at Washington without him. They wondered what their future would be.

3. Arthur Campbell, a Seattle attorney, and H. W. McCurdy are believed to be the only two men still living who were coached by Conibear.

4

Building Airplanes at the Red Barn

Early in 1916, prior to Dr. Suzzallo's overthrow of the University of Washington coaches, George and Dick Pocock had an interesting visitor at the old Tokyo Tea Room. George recalled the meeting, which was to have a major impact on his career:

One afternoon the University president came into the old Tokyo Tea Room with a gentleman we didn't recognize. "These are the boys I was telling you about, Bill," he said. We had a newly finished eight in the shop awaiting shipment to the University of California. Bill Whoever-he-was got under the boat and spent some time on his knees inspecting it with apparent interest. "This is the kind of work I want," he observed to Dr. Suzzallo, who by that time was at the door, tapping the floor with his cane and saying, "Come on, Bill. I must go." Emerging from under the shell, Bill took out his card case, dropped a business card on the workbench, and said, "Come and see me as soon as you can." We looked at the card to see who Bill was; the card read *W. E. Boeing, Hoge Building, Seattle.*

They had heard vaguely of this young scion of a wealthy family with large ore and timber holdings in Minnesota, who had come west in search of opportunities to make his own fortune.

Along the way, he had become an early-day airplane buff, rarely missing one of the big international air meets of those pioneering days. By the time he met the Pococks, he had already acquired timber lands, outfitted expeditions to Alaska, and bought a small shipyard on the Duwamish River to complete a seagoing yacht, the *Taconite,*

52

The Red Barn, 1917 (photo courtesy of the Boeing Company, #P28)

which hadn't been coming along to his satisfaction. He made his first actual flight when a barnstorming pilot named Terah Maroney brought a cloth-and-wire Curtiss-type hydroplane to Seattle. After that there was no stopping Bill Boeing.

On a trip to California, he learned to fly under the tutelage of Glenn L. Martin, and returned with a flimsy biplane on floats, acquired from Martin's modest aircraft factory.

When the Martin seaplane was damaged, Boeing conferred with his friend Conrad Westerveldt, a fellow aviation enthusiast and naval engineer who had helped work out the problems of the *Taconite*. Facing a long delay and considerable cost for the replacement parts Martin needed, Westerveldt observed, "We could build a new plane a hell of a lot better than that one." Boeing agreed, and the eighty-foot-long boatyard shed on the Duwamish (known affectionately for years as "The Red Barn" and now the focal point of a major Seattle aerospace museum) was converted to an airplane manufacturing plant.

When Boeing made his brief visit to the Pocock brothers' shop, his new enterprise was involved with its first project, two "B & W" (for Boeing and Westerveldt) seaplanes, which were eventually sold to New Zealand.

At the time of Boeing's visit to their shop, the Pocock brothers had promised to go to Oakland to do some work for Ben Wallis, the crew coach at the University of California, and then to Redwood City, where shells were being built, to give a helping hand to Husky Gurenna, the Stanford coach. They didn't return to Seattle until after Christmas 1916. By then, of course, Conibear was dead and things had changed radically on the University of Washington rowing scene. Furthermore, it looked more and more likely that the United States would be drawn into the European war, further disrupting life as they had known it. They had wisely kept Bill Boeing's card.

Like Boeing, George had had early contact with man's pioneer efforts to conquer the skies. As a youth at Eton, he and Dick had coached many young men in the fine art of sculling. One of these was a twenty-one-year-old named Tom Sopwith, with whom George spent many hours on the Thames. One summer day in 1909, George and his boyhood chum Jimmy Ottrey were taking a Sunday walk along the river. Coming to Datchet Golf Course, they saw a strange winged contrivance of stick, wire, and muslin taxiing back and forth. They were amazed to find that its occupant was young Tom Sopwith, teaching himself to fly.

George was to learn that Sopwith was a sort of renaissance man of sports, fascinated by all its aspects. By 1910, he had not only taught himself to fly, but had won the de Forest Prize for the longest European flight. In 1914 he had designed and built the seaplane that won the Schneider Trophy. He later became an avid yachtsman, building and sailing the *Endeavor I* and *Endeavor II* to contend for the America's Cup. His Sopwith Aviation Company Ltd., formed in 1912, produced the fabled Sopwith Camel fighter planes of World War I, and his successor company built the Hurricane fighters and Lancaster bombers of World War II, as well as the first British jet, the Gloster E 28/39.

Unlike Boeing and Sopwith, George had no desire to try the skies in the flimsy early planes. Aviation might be the wave of the future, but it was a poor second choice for the sons of generations of traditional watermen and boatbuilders.

Still, with Conibear gone and the University of Washington crew in limbo, it might be the only choice they had. So in early January 1917, George recorded, "we went to see Mr. W. E. Boeing. He seemed glad to see us, and said he would like us to build two sets of pontoons for his seaplanes. It seemed the conventional seaplane floats then in use were so heavy that they seriously hampered the planes' performance. He said his chief engineer, Jim Foley, would bring the plans and show us what he

George Pocock (front cockpit) in the float plane built for the Navy at Boeing

wanted. He did so, and it looked to be an interesting little job. After all, they were to be built of wood, and they weren't much different from small boats.

"Foley asked what we thought they would weigh, since that was such a major factor. We told him 'about 115 pounds each.' He said, 'If you can build them that light I'll buy you each a new hat.' When we finished the first pair, one weighed 114 pounds; the other 116. We never did get the hats, though."

The United States was, of course, drawn into the war shortly thereafter, and the Boeing Airplane Company received its first quantity order—for fifty of the twin-float seaplanes. Of this first government order for Boeing-built aircraft, George recalled:

> The company had sent a prototype back to Pensacola, Florida, for Navy testing, and the results weren't too complimentary. There were a number of faults they said had to be corrected, but what didn't hurt our feelings was the comment on the floats or pontoons: "A very workmanlike job." The order for fifty Boeing "C-Type" planes required a total of 150 pontoons, half of them spares. We couldn't possibly begin a job of that magnitude in the old Tokyo Tea Room on the campus, so we moved our operations to the famous old "Red Barn" on the Duwamish River, which had first been converted from boat to

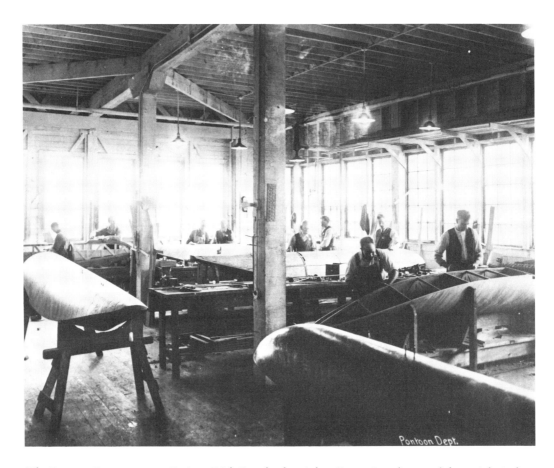

The Pontoon Department at Boeing; Dick Pocock, far right; George Pocock, second from right (photo courtesy of the Boeing Company, #P40)

aircraft building under the name Pacific Aero Products Company. We hired a dozen men who, with Dick and me, were soon turning out a pair of pontoons a day. Not very impressive in this day of assembly line procedures, but considered high-speed production in 1917.

We had taken out our preliminary papers for American citizenship, and we registered for the draft of course. My name came up on the first drawing, and I was ordered to report for a pre-induction physical examination. I duly reported at the Seattle Police Department's Wallingford precinct station, and joined the line of young men called by the draft board. When my turn came, the doctor noted the two missing fingers on my right hand, the result of my old injury at the Vancouver shipyard. He said, "I guess this gets you an exemption." I looked pleased, held out my hand and said, "Shake, Doc." I gave him a grip that caused him to wince a bit. It seemed that the strength of the lost fingers had gone into the others; an instance of nature compensating. I laughed

*The crew of the Assembly Department: Dick Pocock (*sixth from left*), George Huckle (*seventh from left*), Hilmar Lee (*eleventh from left*), George Pocock (*eighth from right*), W. E. Boeing (*third from right*)*

and told him I didn't want an exemption, and he agreed I didn't seem to need one after all.

In a short time I received notice to report to Fort Lewis for induction into the service, but the day before I was to report, a General Crowder, head of the national draft, visited the Boeing shop and stood watching me work for a few minutes. Finally he said, "I see you are to go and prepare to fight the Germans." I replied, "Sir, I will be proud to go." In a voice that brooked no argument, he said, "No you will not! You can be of far more use to the war effort right where you are." I may not have had army training, but I knew enough not to argue with a man wearing as many stars as he was. "As you wish, sir," I said, refraining at the last moment from saluting smartly.

"Phew!" I told myself when he had left. "Boeing goes right to the top men."

The Pocock brothers and their crew had the 150 pontoons built before a single airframe was assembled. The production manager then sent George over to act as foreman of the final assembly plant. Skilled craftsman that he was, it didn't take him long to see why progress was so slow, and to take corrective action:

"I saw that every part was made precisely the same in every way; then fastened on with bolts and castellated nuts. The workman would then take a *hand-drill* and slowly bore a hole through the nickel steel bolt for a cotter key to prevent the nut from loosening. A frightful waste of time!

"I made a chart with all the distances of bolt holes and had the bolts pre-drilled in the machine shop. The airframes started rolling out in fine shape, and the men's morale went way up, now they could see themselves accomplishing so much more."

With more efficient assembly methods, the completion of the first government contract was soon in sight, and George was sent to New York to meet Boeing, who would get him credentials to visit any aircraft plant in the country. He was to tour the plants and report what he learned to the Boeing plant in Seattle. George recalled his New York meeting with Bill Boeing vividly:

> I met Mr. Boeing at the Biltmore Hotel, and he took me by taxi to the Navy Office Temporary in New York. We were there at least an hour while all the proper signatures and stamps were affixed to my credentials, and all this time the taxi was waiting with its meter ticking. I was still accustomed to five-cent streetcar rides and considered a taxi ride something of a luxury. When my credentials were in hand, Mr. Boeing said he had more business to transact at the Navy Office and that I should head directly for the first plant on my list, the College Point Boat Corporation at College Point, Long Island. "You take a train from Penn Station," he directed. "You can take that taxi that is waiting, and discharge it when you get to the station." I had to pay the bill, which was over $15. In that day it seemed to me a big item to start my expense sheet with.

Boeing's next contract was to be for fifty H.S.-2 flying boats, so called because their fuselages were built like boat hulls to provide the flotation which the light Pocock-built pontoons had given to the earlier class of seaplanes. George accordingly scheduled his inspection trips to the plants which were building the flying boats, and his reports to the home office were detailed and frank. He labored over them late into the night after his plant visits were completed, and mailed them before he went to bed. His observations would then be distributed to the various departments concerned at the Boeing plant on the Duwamish.

George found the College Point operation satisfactory, and George Lawley's converted boatyard at Neponset, Massachusetts, "an education; they were doing beautiful work." The Buffalo plant of Curtiss Aircraft: "poor work. Quite inefficient." The Fisher Body Company in Detroit: "a system for sure; progressive production and excellent work."

The Curtiss plant might not have had the most efficient production system in the American aircraft industry of that day, but George found that it had a highly efficient anti-spy network composed of some hundred borrowed New York detectives. As a matter of fact, he was caught for a time in that net, and described his experience in later years:

> I was chatting with the Curtiss plant superintendent, who told me the drawings I had looked at weren't up to date. The location of the controls and piping to the engines in the cockpit had been changed. He said I could get into a finished plane and sketch the new layout.
>
> I did so, and shortly afterward a head rose over the plane's side and a suspicious voice demanded to know what I was doing. I told him I was making a sketch of the controls. "Who for?" he asked, obviously more suspicious than ever. "The Boeing Company, Seattle," I replied. "Never heard of them. Where are your credentials?" I showed him my U.S. Navy authorization papers, but they didn't seem to do much to lull his suspicions. "You better come with me," he ordered. I got out and went with him to an office where a uniformed New York police lieutenant was seated at a desk.
>
> My plain-clothed detective said he had found me in one of the ships "copying stuff," and that I claimed to be from an outfit called Boeing, which he had never heard of. He handed my credentials to his superior, who scanned them, mumbling "Boeing. Boeing. I never heard of them either." Finally he took up the telephone and called someone, apparently of higher authority. I could hear a rapid chatter from the phone, the police officer put it down with an "O.K., sir," took my paper, scrawled "O.K., Sweeney" across it and, "Do what you like," he said, handing it back to me. My captor looked a bit crestfallen. I guess he was sure he had nabbed a German spy.

Of one thing George was certain, that "we had far better material for planking these flying boat hulls than the white pine all the East Coast plants were using. That material was vertical grain western red cedar. It is the wood eternal. It never rots. It does not shrink in opposite weather conditions, wet or dry. Western red cedar (*Thuja plicata*) is lighter too. I knew it would make a far better hull and the Navy, after much correspondence, agreed to let us use it as planking for the Boeing H.S.-2 hulls."

George returned to Seattle in time to supervise construction and, as usual, his judgment proved well founded. Boeing was credited by the Navy with building the best H.S.-2 hulls at far less cost than other plants. The giant Curtiss plant, with 14,000 people on its payroll, took 2,400 man-hours to complete a plane. Boeing made them in 900 hours.

But the Boeing order was cut in half when, on "the eleventh day of the eleventh month," November 11, 1918, Germany capitulated, an armistice was signed in a French railway coach, and "the war to end all wars" ended. The work force at Boeing's infant aircraft plant was reduced to about thirty of the more skilled people, mostly carpenters and boatbuilders. To hold this small nucleus together, Boeing did what it did many years later in the early 1970s, when the lack of expected sales for 747 jets and cancellation of the supersonic transport program resulted in the layoff of some 30,000 employees. It sought diversified nonaviation products to build. The woodworking shop built umbrella stands, telephone booths, hat racks, library tables, and even bedroom suites, which proved unprofitable.

The Red Barn went back to being a boatshop. The Boeing Airplane Company was manufacturing something called a "Speed Sea Sled," a scow-bowed boat with an inverted V-bottom and remarkable power and speed as such things were reckoned in the maritime world of 1919. George wrote of this experimental effort:

> Our first sea sled was a 26-footer for Mr. Boeing's personal use. He was at that time courting his future wife, and we knew he was rather anxious to see this one completed so he could take her out joy riding. He used to come quite often to the shop where we building it and watch us work.
>
> One afternoon he was there sitting on a bench, and seemed to be in such good spirits that I thought I would ask him a question which was uppermost in the minds of everyone working for him. I said, "Mr. Boeing, it must be a problem to you to decide what to do with this plant. We know you are spending a great deal of money every week. The boys think every time you show up you have the key to lock the place up."
>
> He replied, "No, it is no problem. I'm prepared to run it like this with the people I now have on the payroll as a nucleus, for another two years, *and after those two years we will never look back.*"
>
> How right he was in his faith and foresight. All his friends were imploring him to quit, lock the place up and cut his losses, but he refused to listen to the prophets of doom. It almost seems that some men are selected . . . divinely or not, who knows . . . to be leaders in their fields. William Boeing was one such man.
>
> In due course, Mr. Boeing's prototype sea sled was finished. With the captain of the yacht *Tacomite* as pilot, Merril Musgrave as engineer, and myself as observer, we took it

The Hickman Sea Sled (photo courtesy of the Boeing Company, Louis S. Marsh Collection, HS1353)

up to Victoria, B.C., on a trial run. The distance from Seattle to the British Columbia capital is about ninety miles. We went up slow and easy, to break in the engine, but came back full bore in just two hours for an overall speed of 45 miles an hour. I observed some minor structural weaknesses at top speed, but these were soon corrected.

We then completed ten more sea sleds, but were only able to sell three of them. The other seven sat gathering dust, but then national prohibition became the law of the land. It dried up the supplies of legal liquor, but not the thirst of millions of Americans. Fast rum-runners began speeding cargoes of illicit whiskey to Puget Sound. Dick suggested to the manager that he place an advertisement in the Sunday papers offering the boats for sale and stressing their high speed (which would make it obvious that they could run circles around any Coast Guard patrol boat on the Sound).

On Monday morning all seven of them were sold, for cash.

Following completion of the sea sled project, the Pocock brothers took themselves off the Boeing payroll while they built a pair of eight-oared shells in the building constructed for assembly of the H.S.-2 flying boats. The building was otherwise empty.

No planes of any kind were being built, although the engineering staff (three men and one woman) kept busy designing a couple of models. As George recalled it, those two racing shells probably helped Boeing to get back into the airplane business:

> About this time, a House Committee from Washington, D.C., arrived at the Boeing plant. They were on a nationwide tour of wartime aircraft plants, apparently to determine which ones were worthy of being given government contracts to help them stay in business. They inspected the entire plant: machine shops, plating shop, wing room, woodworking department and, finally, the huge (as we thought then) final assembly building. There was really nothing for them to see except some design drawings and the partly completed models . . . until they made their final stop.
>
> There lay the gleaming new shells, sixty feet long, but still lost in such a big empty place. One member of the committee spotted them and hurried over to inspect them more closely. "Who on earth built these?," he asked Edgar Gott, the general manager. "Oh, two of the boys who work for us," he answered. The committeeman said, "I rowed at Harvard, and I never expected to see anything like this out here. I would like to meet the builders and talk to them." So we were sent for and a pleasant chat ensued— about rowing, not airplanes. By then, all eight members of the committee were studying the boats and expressing admiration for the workmanship, which we thought ourselves was pretty good. Mr. Gott knew an opening when he saw one and told the committee, "That's the kind of workmen we have here." It couldn't have done any harm, as very shortly afterward the company received an order for 200 pursuit planes and, as William Boeing had predicted, *they never looked back*."

George did look back in his memoirs, though, hoping to provide "a bit of life and color to the formative years of what has become the world's greatest aircraft manufacturing firm."

> In the early days, Mr. Boeing used to host a monthly dinner for all officers and supervisory employees. It was held at the College Club in Seattle. Mr. Boeing always ceremoniously designated who would sit at his right, and who at his left. His words were, "Mr.———, I must inflict myself on you to my right, and Mr.———, I must inflict myself on you to my left." Different people in the places of honor each month. When my turn came to sit at his right, I carried it off fairly well until the after-dinner cigars were passed around. I took one and put the wrong end in my mouth as he held the lighter toward it. I guess he sensed that I wasn't much of a smoker, because there was a hint of a twinkle in his eye as he said, "Turn it around my boy. You have the wrong end in your mouth." A case of being overawed by the big boss.
>
> At another of the monthly meetings there were two unusual guests, Captain Eddie Rickenbacker, the famous World War I flying ace, and Professor Kirsten, a University of Washington aeronautics expert. They were both asked to say a few words, and when Professor Kirsten's turn came he informed us that he was designing a wheel covered

with airfoils, each of which took a different angle of incidence as the wheel revolved. This, he assured us, was going to revolutionize flight by air. Since Boeing was spending a half million dollars on his experimental prototype, we all managed to keep straight faces. But then he said the airplane of the future would flap its wings like a bird!

Boeing looked at him aghast, while Eddie Rickenbacker leaned back in his chair and roared with laughter, in which, I am afraid, a number of us joined. Mr. Boeing just sat silently and continued to stare at the Professor incredulously."

George and Dick remained with Boeing until 1922, while the company built and remodeled a wide variety of planes. Then it began work on the first all-steel welded aircraft. It was apparent that wood was on the way out in airplane construction, and the further the shift to metal went, the less the Pocock brothers enjoyed their work.

By this time, although University of Washington crew racing was less than two decades old, it was already beginning to gain fame as the training ground of increasing numbers of major college rowing coaches. Ed Leader, a former Husky oarsman under Conibear, had succeeded to the coaching position after the death of his mentor. Leader's crews had made an excellent showing at the most recent Poughkeepsie Regatta, coming in a close second to Navy. Yale University offered Leader the head coaching job at New Haven. Leader accepted the offer, and asked George to go with him as shell-builder and consultant. George declined.

One reason for his reluctance to leave Seattle was a major change that had just taken place in his life. In August 1922, he married Frances Huckle, the sister of Myron Huckle, one of his workers at Boeing. George's father had always advised him, "Never choose a wife until you are over thirty and have a bit of good sense." The advice appears to have been valid, for George and Frances Pocock remained very much in love for the next fifty-four years.

In regard to Leader's offer, George explained, "Dick was more anxious than I to leave Boeing, and I suggested to Ed that he take Dick along, which he did. Dick spent the rest of his life building boats for Yale, while I kept on at Boeing as a foreman, and I am sure I could have spent the rest of my working life with the company." In the meantime, Lucy Pocock had married James Stillwell, a contractor whose company subsequently built the Montlake Cut. Kathleen also married, and moved to California.

Russell S. (Rusty) Callow, who had rowed on the varsity crew under Conibear and, as student body president, had interceded with President Suzzallo to reinstate his old coach, was named to succeed Leader as crew coach at Washington.

"Rusty came to Boeing to talk to me about building an eight for him," George recalled. "I told him I would, in my spare time and days off, if they could supply a building on campus in which to work on it. The crew quarters were now in the

George and Frances Pocock on their wedding day

hanger which had been built to train pilots in seaplanes and flying boats during the war. It was a lofty building with plenty of space for an upper floor, which Rusty said he would provide. During the time the University was the site of a wartime naval training station, the old Tokyo Tea Room, in which we had built shells from 1912 to 1917, was used as brig (a jail in Navy terms). After the war it underwent long overdue demolition."

The upper level shell-building facility provided by the University had no frills, but it provided a space twenty feet wide and seventy feet long, which was adequate for the construction of eight-oared shells. Primitive and unfinished as it was, George felt he could make it do, since he had no intention of throwing away the financial security, seniority, and excellent work record he had achieved at Boeing. The crew-house loft would be used for spare-time pursuit of a modestly popular and much loved hobby.

But fate and a *Seattle Post-Intelligencer* writer had other things in store for him. A story in the sports section was boldly headlined, "POCOCK TO BUILD SHELLS AGAIN ON UNIVERSITY CAMPUS."

George felt that he had been forced into a situation with only one alternative. "I just could not stay with Boeing," he wrote, "because a man cannot split his loyalties. In my case it involved, in the words of the poet, 'forsaking the substance and grasping the shadow.'

"On December 22, 1922, I left the Boeing Airplane Company and started anew in my old love, boatbuilding."

5

"Clumsily Built Western Boats"

GEORGE POCOCK had, indeed, "forsaken the substance and grasped the shadow." The contrast between the security and comfortable working conditions at the Boeing plant, and the cold, bare loft on the university campus "was really ghastly." It was midwinter when he made the change and the shop, he recalled, was "cold, very very cold." Some radiators were installed, but the steam seemed unable to reach the height necessary to warm them. The shop space was bare as well as cold. Building stocks, workbenches, shelves, storage areas, all would have to be built before work could be started on the first shell.

"In the months that followed," he recorded, "I lay awake nights, convinced that I had made the mistake of my life in leaving Boeing; from foreman over sixty men to working alone in a garret workshop. I worked long hours, often not getting home until eight or nine o'clock at night. With no capital to speak of to buy machinery, it was all hard handwork."

His greatest asset during that trying and somewhat frightening period was the young bride he had so recently taken. "Frances, my wonderful helpmate, never complained," he recalled, "whereas I am sure many women would have insisted on the security we enjoyed when I was on the Boeing payroll. She would invariably meet me with a smile and warm food when I came home late, cold and more than a little discouraged. She was, I realized more than ever, the light of my life."

Rusty Callow also proved to be a true friend and a tower of strength during that trying time. "He was a true Christian gentleman," George wrote. "I put my trust in

University of Washington shell house, 1920s

him from the beginning because I had to, but I soon found that it was well founded. Rusty Callow was a truly honorable man, in the old-fashioned sense of that term."

The relationship between the two men became a blending of professional teamwork and close friendship, bound by mutual respect. Rusty's father had migrated from the almost treeless slate cliffs of the Isle of Man to raise a family of seven sons and four daughters on a homestead he had hacked from the mighty rain forests of the Olympic Peninsula. Once a year the numerous Callow brothers would assemble at some spot in the Peninsula wilderness, pack in supplies for the hired cook, and invite all their friends to attend this all-male conclave, for a day or two or a full fortnight. All they had to do was bring their own blankets. The result was a joyful gathering of what was to George, who soon joined the chosen ones, an amazing mix of doctors, lawyers, clergymen, political figures, loggers, and laborers. Such a fellowship would have been inconceivable in late Victorian and Edwardian England, where he had spent his formative years. He and Dick hadn't even been permitted to row in "gentlemen's races,"

Russell S. "Rusty" Callow, varsity crew coach, University of Washington, 1922–27; University of Pennsylvania, 1927–50; U.S. Naval Academy, 1951–59

since they were of the working class, and working men of course could be expected to have more muscle than sons of the gentry and aristocracy.

The gathering was totally unstructured. The campers did whatever they wanted to, but George also noted that none seemed to choose the "blood sports" so favored by the British upper classes. They seemed to feel a kinship with the beautiful animals who shared the wilderness paradise with them, and had no urge to kill them. At night, all assembled about a roaring campfire to swap tall tales, all comrades in what George called "the leveling of the Great Outdoors." Sometimes a man would take over from the paid cook to demonstrate his culinary specialty. Bob Callow was famous for his clam chowder. Rusty would make a long hike to the seashore to return with a huge sack of oysters, which he would broil in their juices on top of the red-hot camp stove. Flavored with a bit of vinegar, they were in George's memory, "food for the gods."

That band of brothers and their chosen friends all seemed bigger than life, but Rusty's older brother, Ted Callow, impressed George most. He had made his living as a logger, but he was determined to become a doctor. He worked longer and harder than ever and began saving enough money to support his wife and children during the long years of medical training. He was forty years old before he felt sure they had enough. Then he entered medical school and eventually became a practicing physician and surgeon. "What ambition! What character!" George reflected in later years. "Doctor Ted was truly a giant in those days."[1]

It was as a member of that brotherhood of the forest that English-born George Pocock learned the true meaning of the words of the Declaration of Independence, which he had been required to learn as a requisite to American citizenship, "that all men are created equal."

But he could never quite rid himself of the British class consciousness, any more than he could entirely lose his British accent, with its Etonian overtones. His son, Stan, recalled a visit many years later to the then-famous Pocock boatshop by a member of the Nixon administration. To George, he was a minister of state and he greeted him with the humility he had been taught was proper for a member of the working class toward such an exalted personage. Stan still remembers how exasperated he was:

---

1. Gordon Callow, Rusty's son, has kindly added these details regarding the annual forest retreat: "The original Callow brothers' 'week in the Olympics' had only the seven brothers and four brothers-in-law. It gradually expanded to include upwards of sixty people. Bill Grisdale, Simpson Timber Company logging superintendent and a brother-in-law, did most of the cooking. My father said, 'Those that wanted to play bridge (notably Dr. Ted) did so; those that wanted to fish did; those who wanted to sleep, slept; those who wanted to tell stories did so; and those who wanted to holler hollered.'"

"I knew my father was as good a man as any politician and a good deal better than most. It riled me to see him treating this guy like some kind of superior being."

Back at his makeshift shop in the winter of 1922, George was faced with the need to build essential equipment before he could begin making shells for Rusty Callow. After counting his slim financial resources, he placed a modest order for materials with Walter Way, the foreman of the Boeing woodworking shop. In due time, a truck pulled up at the hanger with a capacity load of milled spruce lumber.

"It was at least four times what I had ordered," he recalled, "and when the bill arrived I was almost too scared to open it, convinced the cost would be more than I could possibly pay. When I finally got my courage up, I saw to my surprise and joy that the total was only $90. I knew it was worth at least $500. I immediately got Walter Way on the phone and thanked him. He replied, 'Mostly good will you know, George.' The old Biblical verse was proving true again: the one about casting your bread upon the waters. Walter had been one of our old gang of twelve who built those first seaplane floats. I had hired him in the first place and boosted him up along the way to the foreman's position he then held. This was his way of saying thanks, and giving *me* a boost up."

By early 1923 the first new shell was completed, designated *Husky,* and prepared for rail shipment to Poughkeepsie, where Husky crews had been trying for ten years to win that most prestigious of American college regattas. This time George didn't have to read the race results in the Seattle papers. He was there in person, at the urging of Rusty Callow. Along the way, the Washington entourage stopped off at Madison, Wisconsin, where Hiram Conibear's daughter, Katherine, officially christened the gleaming new shell by breaking a bottle of Lake Washington water over its prow. The varsity oarsmen who held the boat looked on with apprehension as to how the fragile-looking shell would withstand the blow. George knew all along that it would come out very well, and it did.

The Husky freshmen also came out well at Madison, proudly stroking the *Husky* in its maiden race to a clear victory over the University of Wisconsin frosh.

After touring the Wisconsin capitol the Washingtonians boarded the train for Chicago, where they would transfer to a crack express train, the New York Central, for Poughkeepsie. At the Chicago station they were met by Dr. Alfred Strauss, a University of Washington alumnus and one of the Windy City's most distinguished surgeons. He had a fleet of taxis waiting for them, and George was somewhat awed by what proved to be his first taste of VIP treatment: "Headed and trailed by traffic policemen, we sped through the heart of Chicago toward the Lincoln Park Boat Club with sirens continually blaring. I do not know which were the most goggle-eyed, the people on

Hiram Conibear's daughter, Katherine, christens the varsity shell Husky, *Lake Mendota, Wisconsin, June 1923*

the streets or our people in the cabs, most of whom had never been outside the state of Washington. What an experience for them! And, I must admit, for me too."

The westerners found the express to Poughkeepsie an interesting contrast to the trains they were used to: faster, less friendly, and much more formal. When the young oarsmen entered the dining car in T-shirts and sweaters, they were met by a scandalized steward who sent them back to don coats and ties. "Which decorum," George recorded with a trace of British primness, "is really commendable."

They found things less formal, and certainly less elegant, at the quarters assigned to them in Poughkeepsie. Keith Middleton, the crew manager, had received a telegram along the way from Mayor Peter Troy of that city informing him that VIP quarters had been reserved for the varsity crew, the freshmen to be housed separately in presumably less elegant surroundings. One bit of information in the telegram had provided a note of warning: "We have provided plenty of oil for the lamps." George recalled their arrival at Poughkeepsie:

. . . we unloaded the shells and coaching launch from the shell car, along with five stowaways, who had made the trip hidden in the launch. The shell car was spotted at the Dutton Lumber Company yard, where Halsey Wykoff, a former Washington oarsman and general manager of the company, was there to greet us. He had a crew of his men on hand to move the coaching launch to the river, while we, along with the oarsmen, carried the shells onto the ferry steamer *Governor Clinton,* which transported men, boats, and bags across the Hudson River to the Highland side.

After stowing the shells in one of the riverside shacks, we walked along the river road to the Vrooman House. It not only had oil lamps in place of electricity, but dirt floors as well. Its principal article of furniture was a massive old four-poster bed upstairs, for which there was a lively scramble. I think Harry John Dutton and Harrison Sanford got it, but it was a hollow victory to say the least.

One night and one meal was enough. The following morning it was found that the four-poster had already been occupied . . . by bedbugs. Dozens of them. Harry Dutton and Stork Sanford were a long time ridding themselves of their bite scars. The varsity was then moved up to Mrs. Palmer's house on the hill at Highland, where everything was clean and Mrs. Palmer served excellent food.

I got down to the shell shack early and rigged our shells. Soon afterward, down came the boys, full of high spirits despite the dilapidated condition of the building and its total lack of amenities: no running water for showers, no dressing rooms. It was intended for rugged individuals, which our men proved to be. We improvised a shower, but had to pump water from the river. I had doubts about its cleansing qualities, since the Hudson received raw sewage and industrial waste from every city along its course.

During the ten days of pre-race training, our boys had a lot of fun with the crusty old chap who was rigger for Navy, who shared our shell shack. They were always assured of a blistering counter-attack when they referred to his shell as "The Navy Log." It was all in fun of course, and I think old Mr. Kantler of Navy secretly enjoyed it too. Rusty Callow had a rare ability to retain the respect of his crews and maintain the rigorous discipline needed for a successful team effort without killing their spirit; rather, he raised it. He was a coach who never swore at his men, but would crack jokes from the launch, making them all laugh and then work even harder for him. I know it's an overworked term, but Rusty Callow was in truth a real leader of men if ever there was one.

The evening before race day, the shells were rowed up the river to the Columbia boathouse, which was a permanent masonry structure with good accommodations, located about a quarter of a mile from the starting line. The two-mile freshman race came first, and Washington quite obviously nosed out second place Cornell, although by a scant margin. In fact, the Cornell crew had acknowledged defeat by giving their rowing shirts to the Huskie Pups, the traditional gesture of losing crews, when a launch full of officials (representing all the schools except Washington) came charging up with the announcement that Cornell had won. The Washington oarsmen had to hand over the Cornell shirts, and theirs as well.

It is almost impossible to judge a very close race like this one without a fixed camera at the finish line. Rusty and I had watched from the observation train and were certain that Washington had won, although, good sportsman that he was, Rusty made no comment. But the following week we received a package from *The Literary Digest,* one of many once-famous national publications which have since vanished. They had a camera at the finish line, and the photograph they sent clearly showed that Washington had won. However, the record book shows Cornell as the winner. Sports officials never seem to reverse their decisions, regardless of the evidence.

There were no junior varsity races in those days, so the main event—the varsity race—followed, and this was a tough one all the way. Columbia went off with the lead, followed by Navy, Cornell, Syracuse, Washington, and Wisconsin. Then Navy took the lead and Washington got by Columbia for second place. At the Poughkeepsie Railway Bridge, with a mile to go, Navy shot under the span first, with Washington a very close second, and Cornell third. On the observation train following the race, the excitement was loud and hectic. All the different school supporters, except those for Navy, were now yelling "Come on, Washington!" And come on Washington did, knifing past Navy and crossing the finish line by a big enough margin to leave nothing in doubt.

This was an unprecedented upset, a crew from the Far West soundly beating the best in the East. The easterners were asking, "Where on earth is Seattle? We never heard of it." To further confuse them, we had brought along a supply of very small totem poles to distribute as souvenirs. This convinced them beyond doubt that we surely had come from Indian country.

Everybody loves a winner, and there was much back-slapping and congratulating of the crew and coach. The oarsmen were given their return tickets to Seattle and $125 each as expense money, and were free to choose which route and rail line they would take.

Here I must mention Loyal Shoudy, M.D.; well-named, for he was an intensely loyal Washington alumnus and a former football player under Gil Dobie. He was then head of the medical department of Bethlehem Steel, and was credited with having introduced the specialty of industrial medicine. He had come from Bethlehem, Pennsylvania, to see the race. The result so delighted him that he treated the winning varsity and "losing" freshmen to a gala dinner and stage show in New York, with the further gifts of a purple necktie and a ten-dollar bill at each plate. This became an annual affair with Dr. Shoudy as host, and it remained a tradition of Washington rowing even after the death of the good and generous man who inaugurated it. Each year, following the IRA race, the University of Washington crew coach hosts a Loyal Shoudy Banquet, with purple ties at every place.

Rusty and I stayed on at Poughkeepsie, working at the Dutton Lumber yard to build two crates large enough to hold the eight-oared shells for shipment back to Seattle. Halsey Wykoff, as filled with pride as Dr. Shoudy by the triumph of his *alma mater,* donated all the lumber for the project, and the Luckenbach Steamship Company, which carried Washington lumber to the Dutton yard, transported the shells back to Seattle free of charge.

Rusty and I, dressed in coveralls, worked like mad to get those crates ready in time for the ship's departure. One of the yard workmen came up to me on one occasion and asked in a tone of disbelief, "Is that guy really the coach of the University of Washington crew?" I realized that the rugged democracy I was beginning to get used to in the Far West was still puzzling to people of the more effete East.

With the shells safely on their way, Rusty and I returned home together by way of Duluth, Winnepeg, Edmonton, and Vancouver, taking the familiar Canadian Pacific steamer from Vancouver to Seattle. When we arrived, we were met by a large reception committee, including the mayor, city councilmen, and, first and foremost, our wives. The mayor presented Rusty with a big golden Key to the City. The subsequent wining and dining of the conquering heroes I know nothing of, as I had to get back to work. All my time over the five weeks past had been unpaid.

The trip to Poughkeepsie may have sent George Pocock's cash flow on a downward trend, but in the long run it proved a wise investment. He met the great rowing coaches of that time: Dad Vail of Wisconsin, colorful and crusty Jim Ten Eyck of Syracuse, Charles Courtney of Cornell, Dick Glendon of Navy, and Jim Rice of Columbia. They took to George, and, when Washington swept the course at Poughkeepsie in a Pocock-built shell, they took to the product of his modest boatshop with equal enthusiasm.

Within days of his return, he had orders for eight new eight-oared shells and, like Bill Boeing, "he never looked back."

It was apparent that the days of one-man operations were past. George had cleared the first hurdle on a course that would lead to a virtual monopoly in the United States in the production of fine, hand-crafted racing shells. "I couldn't build that many alone," he wrote, "so I hired men to train in the work and spent all my waking hours on the job. This is where a good wife can be a treasure. Frances understood my aims and encouraged me."

The triumph of the *Husky* at Poughkeepsie had gone far toward convincing coaches that Pocock shells were winners, but the sports writers who covered intercollegiate rowing were a long time in coming to the same conclusion. Sometimes their preconceived opinions gave rise to ridiculous errors in reporting, which George viewed wryly in later years:

> One big prejudice I had to overcome for a decade or more after 1912 was the opinion that anything made west of Chicago had to be inferior. For instance, in 1915 we built a shell for Stanford University. After winning their West Coast races, they were invited to Poughkeepsie for the National Intercollegiate Regatta, but found it would be too expensive to take their Pocock shell with them, as it would require a seventy-foot special baggage car. They borrowed an eastern shell and came in second in the race. A New York newspaper reported: "If Stanford had not been using a clumsily built western shell, they would have won the race."

In another instance, a Harvard crew was swamped on a stormy day on the Charles River Basin in Boston. A Boston newspaper account said, "The Pocock-built shell broke in a thousand pieces." I wrote the coach to ask if it were true. He replied, "No, it was a shell built in England." Such are the prejudices one must overcome.

Ever the philosopher, George noted that "a verse from Longfellow's poem, 'Psalm of Life' gave me a lot of courage: 'Let us then be up and doing, with a heart for any fate, / Still achieving, still pursuing, learn to labor and to wait.'

"So I labored and waited and, twenty years later, every shell in the Poughkeepsie Regatta was a 'western, clumsily built Pocock boat.'

"Thirty of them."

6

"Eight Hearts
Must Beat As One"

THOSE NOT intimately involved in the sport of rowing, if they recognize the name of George Pocock at all, will probably identify him as "the man who built those beautiful shells at the University of Washington." He did indeed build beautiful racing shells, the most beautiful and functional the world had ever seen, but his influence on rowing in the United States went far deeper than the crafting of boats and oars.

As an athlete, he had devoted much of his life to refining the simple premise that superior rowing is the art of making a boat slide through the water at maximum speed with minimum effort. The stroke which swept University of Washington crews to national and international fame in the 1920s and 1930s was, in truth, the Pocock stroke. George was far too modest to claim much credit at the time, but in his memoirs he did admit that he "had quite a bit to do with it." As Washington crews began to produce rowing coaches for major colleges across the nation, the techniques he had a major share in developing spread throughout collegiate rowing in America. In 1972, he put a description of his stroke in writing:

> Before going any further, I think I should describe the stroke Washington was using, as I had quite a bit to do with it. The ex-Washington oarsmen, through the *Seattle Times,* were asked in the 1920s, to select a name for the then famous Washington stroke. As the Conibear-coached alumni were then in the great majority, the name "Conibear Stroke" came into being. Although, in Rusty Callow's words, "Connie never taught the same stroke two years running," nobody should begrudge Connie the name,

76

1925

George Pocock, sculling at Seattle in 1925

for he certainly got rowing off to a grand start at Washington despite the fact he never did learn to row very well himself.

It is very difficult for me to say this, but after all, I had had years of experience rowing and sculling under old-time professionals on the Thames in England. I had never given it up and, in 1923 at the age of 32, I was in pretty good shape. Rusty Callow would get me to row by the crew in my single and tell them to watch the action of squeezing out the finish; coming to an upright position via leverage from the oar blades and *not* pulling via the feet, but having them loose. A smooth turn of the wrists, and the hands away smoothly and quickly. When the arms are straight, the slide moves slowly forward, not slowing the run of the boat. When at full reach, ready for the next stroke, an almost imperceptible hesitancy.

Now here is the point in the stroke that can make or break the run. If you drive the legs too soon, you break the run. If you try to catch the water without moving the slide, you either have to bend the elbows down, or swing the back without moving the slide, which can cause a double stroke. So many crews develop a double stroke; a catch and a finish, which results in drifting over dead center with no pull of the oars. The stroke as described is one which eliminates that costly loss of forward speed, and can be executed in a smooth, one-piece drive.

A good sculler of Thames fame will make these moves simultaneously. He will catch and drive with the legs at the same time, keeping his back in the same position and his arms straight. When the initial drive is at midpoint, he bends his elbows to come faster over dead center, his back slowly comes over to about a thirty-degree layback, his hands squeeze, providing the force to keep the run on as long as possible before taking the next stroke.

These movements are almost impossible to put on paper or explain by word of mouth; they have to be demonstrated with constant practice until the oarsman gets the true "feel" of the boat. It has to literally become a part of him. It is a living thing, and like a spirited horse, it will work well for him if it is handled right. Just as a skilled rider is said to become like part of his horse, the skilled oarsman must become a part of his boat.

George was a firm believer in the adage that "if it's working you shouldn't try to fix it." In his later years he expressed his opinion of new-fangled rowing techniques and shell designs:

> One of the curses of present day rowing and equipment from abroad is the belief that change necessarily implies progress. I am, by birth, nature, and inclination, a traditionalist. I utterly dislike departing from the fundamentals proven over hundreds of years, mainly by professionals who made their living rowing, until I have satisfied myself that the new style offers equally good results. So far I have not been impressed with any of the new departures. I suppose in modern parlance I am a reactionary, but I am only opposed to change if it appears to be change for the worse. When this is the case, I would like to change 'em back again quickly. This applies to a great majority of rowing in America today.

Convinced that a well-rowed racing eight is a thing of beauty and a joy forever, a symphony of coordinated motion, George's heart and soul rebelled at the sight of a clumsy, unskilled crew punishing the graceful craft they were mishandling:

There is no more pitiful sight than a crew abusing a shell, with the boat checking at every stroke and the crew laboring hard—probably too hard—but with little or no skill or artistry. Usually with a double stroke; a catch and a finish. Again I must repeat, it is difficult to express in words what a topnotch crew must feel. Probably "geared to the boat" *might* express it. Tempers must be held in check. I have seen angry and frustrated oarsmen slashing at the water as if trying to break their oars. This does more to stop the run and lose the race. Such men, in the old parlance, are called "stoppers." Good thoughts have much to do with good rowing. It isn't enough for the muscles of a crew to work in unison; their hearts and minds must also be as one. To see a winning crew in action is to witness a perfect harmony in which everything is right; coach, boat and mates. That is the formula for endurance and for success; rowing with the heart and the head as well as physical strength.

Rowing is the world's oldest competitive sport. Superior crews crop up in all countries which practice it, and the common pitfall is trying to copy the successful crew of the moment instead of staying with your own convictions. For example, the United States had dominated Olympic Eights from 1920 to 1960. That year a German crew won the gold against a rather mediocre American entry. The rush began immediately to abandon our good American style and adapt various interpretations of the German style. The result was a long eclipse of the bright sun of American rowing victories. Ironically, a New Zealand crew won the gold medal in 1972, rowing exactly in the style of America's world champions in their heyday.

Another of George's firm convictions held that the enthusiastic support of the news media was essential to a successful college rowing program. This conviction was based on practical considerations:

It may be said that rowing is too often the poor stepchild of university athletic programs, since there is no way that it can generate money to support itself. The University of Washington was most fortunate in the backing given its crews by the Seattle daily newspapers. This literally made it possible to enter the big time national rowing events and the Olympic Games.

The *Seattle Times* was published by Alden J. Blethen, whose son became a varsity coxswain at Washington. An ardent fan himself, Blethen lured a top sports reporter named George Varnell away from the Spokane daily to concentrate his efforts on varsity rowing. The writer from the Inland Empire of dryland eastern Washington took to the water like a duck. After preliminary trips in the coaching launch with Rusty Callow teaching him the fine points of the game, Varnell began writing a daily column on crew activities, which soon became one of the widest-read features in the city's largest newspaper. Too much cannot be said of the important part this played in the success of the crews. Since there were no university funds to send them to out-of-state regattas, George Varnell and the *Times* conducted a public drive for subscriptions to defray travel costs. Husky crews had become Seattle's pride, resulting in such huge donations that the drive had to be stopped after just three days. The amount needed had been oversubscribed.

The morning paper, the *Post-Intelligencer*, became almost as crew-oriented when Royal Brougham became its sports editor. Pre-race newspaper coverage resulted in crowds of 100,000 or more turning out along the shores of Lake Washington to see the crew races in Seattle. The Husky oarsmen became heroes to growing numbers of high school age boys, and there were always numbers of them down to watch the practice turnouts. One could well imagine they were thinking of the day when they could put on purple and gold rowing shirts and pull an oar in a Washington racing shell.

Although good publicity aroused public enthusiasm and resulted in successful fund drives to send Washington crews to national and international competitions, the day-to-day, bread-and-butter survival of a successful crew program depended also upon the generosity of a relatively small number of rowing aficionados like Dr. Loyal Shoudy, who were willing and able to contribute money for such essentials as buildings, new shells, training tables, and coach's travel. To George, the most enthusiastic and dedicated oarsman of them all, this group was made up of "men and women superior in mind and action . . . an indispensable breed" and—modestly, as always—"I am not in that category, but to me they are the Royalty of America."

Among the men he mentioned were Horace Davenport of Columbia, Clifford ("Tip") Goes of Syracuse, John L. Collyer of Cornell, Dean Witter of California, Loyal Shoudy of Washington, Francis Lee Higinson and Robert Herrick of Harvard, and H. W. McCurdy, who has generously supported rowing both at Washington, where he rowed on the freshman crew under Conibear, and at MIT, where he captained the varsity crew.

Horace Davenport summed up their motivation: "I got more of the lessons of life from crew than I got from classes, and I want to put something back for it."

For years, George and Rusty Callow chuckled at the recollection of one of their early meetings with a member of this "Rowing Establishment," recounted by George at a Seattle banquet on his 82nd birthday:

> Rusty and I were at Syracuse in the early days of the IRA competition there. We visited the crews' dressing room at the New York State Fair Grounds, and Rusty spotted an old gentleman picking up towels. He looked as if he might be an old city employee assigned to that kind of menial work. Kind-hearted Rusty said to me, "Look at that poor old guy picking up the towels." He went over to him and tried to tip him fifty cents.
>
> Well, that "poor old guy" turned out to be Jim Stimson, the retired Chairman of the Board of Crucible Steel Corporation, and one of the racing stewards. Many a night after that at the stewards' banquets in Syracuse, Jim Stimson and I used to sit together and laugh over that episode.

ROWING A RACE IS AN ART NOT A FRANTIC SCRAMBLE.
IT MUST BE ROWED WITH HEAD POWER AS WELL AS
MUSCULAR POWER.
FROM THE FIRST STROKE ALL THOUGHTS OF THE
OTHER CREW MUST BE BLOCKED OUT.
YOUR THOUGHTS MUST BE DIRECTED TO YOU
AND YOUR OWN BOAT, ALWAYS POSITIVELY, NEVER
NEGATIVE.
ROW YOUR OPTIMUM POWER EVERY STROKE, TRY AND
INCREASE THE OPTIMUM.
MEN AS FIT AS YOU, WHEN YOUR EVERY DAY STRENGTH
IS GONE, CAN DRAW ON A MYSTERIOUS RESERVIOR
OF POWER FAR GREATER. THEN IT IS YOU CAN
REACH FOR THE STARS.
THAT IS THE ONLY WAY CHAMPIONS ARE MADE.
THAT IS THE LEGACY ROWING CAN LEAVE YOU.
DON'T MISS IT.
GOOD LUCK
George Pocock

Pocock's message to the Washington crew on their trip to Henley, 1958, written on the paper that wrapped the oars and discovered by the rowers when they arrived at Henley

Despite the uncomfortable pews at his childhood church on Shepperton Green, George remained a devout Christian throughout his life; one who not only went through the motions of church attendance, but practiced the Ten Commandments and the Golden Rule in his daily life. But hand in hand with his Christian beliefs was an almost mystical devotion to a sort of second religion: rowing.

His mission was to teach young oarsmen how to propitiate and work in harmony with the deities imprisoned in wood and water, and to preach his philosophy of the calling to which he had devoted his life. This he did across the nation in talks described by aging oarsmen as among the most inspirational they have ever heard.

He firmly believed that rowing was the finest builder of character of any sport, involving as it does the most rigorous discipline, great endurance, intense concentration, and total self control. He saw in it the basis for success in most areas of human endeavor—a willingness to pool one's strength in a common cause.

It is interesting to note, in support of his theories in this regard, that, according to statistics compiled by present Washington Crew Coach Dick Erickson, college oarsmen attain by far the highest grade point average of all varsity athletes, and they tend to be enrolled in academic, business, and professional courses rather than less demanding majors.

George also believed strongly that "high schools which are situated anywhere near water are missing the finest training young people can get for becoming good citizens, by not participating in a rowing program."

Competitive rowing had been a high school sport in England long before it was taken up by universities, and in earlier years, British college crews had been dominant. Following the glory days of American college rowing in the 1920s and 1930s, amateur crews from Australia and New Zealand began taking international honors. George found one answer to their success when he visited Australia in later years: "I visited a regatta in Melbourne for high school oarsmen exclusively. There were no less than 1,300 Australian high school boys competing in the events."

In later years George became much in demand as a speaker at crew-related events across the nation. One of many was the dedication of the Hunter S. Marston Boathouse at Brown University in 1967. George was always happy at any opportunity to spread his rowing philosophy—the development of mind, body and character. It also warmed his heart to learn that Brown was one of the first universities in the United States to adopt rowing as a varsity sport. Tradition meant much to him, and he could overlook the fact that the university's early efforts, begun in 1857, were both brief and inglorious. In the first regatta, rowed against Ivy League foes Harvard and Yale, the Brown oarsmen struggled to move their heavy, cumbersome shell, and came in a poor third.

At Syracuse, ca. 1960. From left: Loren Schoel, Rusty Callow, George Pocock, Vic Michaelson

The next year they returned gamely with a lighter shell, which sank under them in mid course. Rowing died a lingering death at Brown, finally expiring in 1875.

But the important thing to George was that, after numerous heartbreaking failures, it was finally brought back to life in 1949, mainly through the dedication of an undergraduate named Jim Donaldson, who passed the hat and raised enough money to buy a second-hand eight-oared shell from a school in Delaware. Donaldson then brought the sixty-one-foot shell back to the Seekonk River, lashed on top of his seventeen-foot coupe.

That was the kind of determination George could appreciate.

The sport made a gradual comeback over the next few years, and in 1961 regained full varsity status and its first full-time coach, Vic Michaelson, a highly successful freshman coach at Syracuse and, like so many others of his profession, a former University of Washington oarsman. Within five years the Brown crew, once known in rowing circles as "the Orphans of the Seekonk," had attained that status of rowing success, an invitation to the Henley Regatta on George's beloved Thames.

Furthermore, the handsome new crewhouse which was being dedicated had been a gift of one of those members of his "Royalty of America," the loyal and wealthy alumni who gave generously to support the last of the true amateur sports. Hunter S. Marston was a Brown graduate of 1908 and head of major eastern banks and corporations.

All in all, it was the sort of occasion that warmed the cockles of George's heart, and his dedication address rose to the occasion. Part paean and part homily, delivered in simple words touched with his soft English accent, it lost his unique personal touch when it was reproduced verbatim in the *Brown Alumni Monthly*, but it remains uniquely Pocockian:

Rowing has been in our family for some time—really. I'm the third generation of lifetimes given to rowing. I was apprenticed under my father at Eton College, England, where he was manager of rowing and head boatbuilder.

There at Eton they looked upon rowing as the most important physical activity (they still do, of course). To prove the point, I have only to mention that they have 650 boats for 1,100 boys. People hear that statement and think it's exaggeration, but it isn't. They have seasons of rowing, you see: they start with eights and then they shift to fours, and go on to the pairs. After the pairs, they have the singles; when that happens, you can walk across the river, almost, on singles.

But rowing and education, training the mind and training the body, are very necessary. And the lessons of rowing are great. It's been called an advanced sport. It isn't advanced in the way of orbiting the earth, but in developing the whole man.

You know, a liberal definition of the word rowing is overcoming difficulties. The opposite of rowing is drifting—and who wants that? I'm not a linguist by any means, but my wife and I, while down in South America a few years ago, found that the word for rowing and struggle there are the same: *"riman."* It rather surprised us that such a thing should be, but there it was: *riman* and rowing. . . .

Now what are these virtues of rowing that make it so important? When Britain was trying to keep the world in order, those men who rowed at Eton went out and really governed the Empire. Today the United States has taken over the role of trying to keep the world in order, and it takes some good men to do it. They have to be trained well; they have to be capable of overcoming terrible difficulties.

There are three things I like to think of as very necessary in life, and they are a part of the rowing game. The first one is harmony. In a squad, you cannot have a crew without harmony. The men have got to like each other. There can't be any culls (that's a fierce word), there can't be any culls in the squad. The men have got to like each other. Eight hearts have to beat as one.

When you're in a crew, you put everything you've got into it, and it takes eight men to do it. If the eight men don't do it, one man gets it all—or two or three, and it's tough on them. Harmony is the most important thing. If there's any friction at all, you might as well say good-bye to your crew.

The second thing is balance. You're on pinpoint balance in an eight-oared shell. It's only 24 inches wide, 10 inches deep, and weighs 280 pounds; you cannot refute the laws of balance in a boat. There are ten motions that have to be performed simultaneously in an eight-oared boat. If you miss any one of them, the whole crew is out of balance—the least little thing will put it out. You've got to have your hands all on one plane, you've got to catch right at the same time, you've got to pull through, you've got to slide, you've got to drive your legs down, you've got to turn a wrist—all at exactly the same time.

It's a beautiful thing to watch when it's done right. The top crew at present is New Zealand's. I have a letter from a coach who said it is an inspiration to watch this New Zealand crew. They weren't really big men. Only two men in the boat were big, and the others were run-of-the-mill. But my friend said they were an inspiration to watch, the way they rowed that boat all together.

Do I make myself clear about the timing that is involved in rowing? It's pretty elementary, but suppose the eight men in a boat were eight golfers at a tee. Line them up, one behind the other, and make them bring their clubs up to exactly the same height, swing and hit the ball with the sound of but one crack. Eight men hitting that golf ball with one crack—that's what a crew has to do when it hits that water. You've got to hit it with one crack, or the boat will not respond.

A boat is a sensitive thing, an eight-oared shell, and, if it isn't let go free, it doesn't work for you. But, honestly—if you get that balance right, then the third thing you get is rhythm. And, when you get that rhythm in an eight, it's pure pleasure to be in it. It's not hard work when the rhythm comes—that swing as they call it. I've heard men shriek out with delight when that swing came in an eight; it's a thing they'll never forget as long as they live.

I've wondered what it is. Well, here's my interpretation of it: I think you have hit perfection when you get swing in a boat. And when you hit perfection you're getting near the divine. I heard Marian Anderson out in Seattle—that's where we're from—in the Civic Auditorium. They've got a good one now, but it was an old barn when she was there; it held, I think, six thousand people. She sang "Ave Maria," and you could have heard a pin drop. It was near the divine. You get the same thing really in a good piece of workmanship: Chippendale furniture, a carving by Gibbons, or something like that. It's really delightful.

And the oarsman, too, when he has his mind trained at the university and his body fit, feels something that reminds me of a bit from Browning: "How good is man's life,

The Husky crew at Henley, 1958. From left: Bob Svendsen, Dick Erickson, Gene Phillips, Phil Kieburtz, Chuck Alm, Lou Gellermann, Andy Hovland, John Sayre, John Bisset

the mere living! How fit to use all the heart and the soul and the senses for the joy of it!''

I think oarsmen understand what I'm talking about. They get that way. I've seen oarsmen—actually I saw one man, who was so rarin' to go, so fit and bright, I saw him try to run up a wall. Now isn't that ridiculous? But he felt that good; he wanted to try and run up that wall.

Of course, I've been an oarsman—my father was, his father was, and now my son. And I'm sure Stan has an advantage over most of the old Pocock lines: he's a graduate engineer. His mother and I didn't encourage him at all to take up boatbuilding. We thought maybe he would like to follow engineering in big work such as bridges, but he chose to come into the shop, and now he's really better than I ever was. It's through him that the business of boatbuilding is going on.

The rowing game is growing by leaps and bounds. One city, Long Beach, California, has ordered 40 shells. When I worked alone, trying to get my roots down, we had two or three institutions on the books; now we have 110 universities and colleges, besides rowing clubs.

But it's the *spirit* of rowing that makes it what it is. In the rowing game, eight hearts must beat as one in an eight-oared shell, or you don't have a crew. And, as I finish, I go back to Browning again for a familiar line but a great one:

"One's reach must exceed his grasp, or what's a heaven for?"

7

"There Are No Fast Boats, Only Fast Crews"

GEORGE'S LOYALTY to the sport of rowing in general was his hallmark throughout his life, but following the Husky crew's surprise victory at Poughkeepsie in 1923, he found that he must assess his loyalties to the University of Washington and to his staunch friend, Rusty Callow.

The dark and doubtful days of his first year on the Lake Washington campus were only memories, and he found himself wooed by a number of prestigious universities around the nation. Harvard made the most pressing overtures. Three members of its rowing committee journeyed to Seattle to offer him many inducements, including a new fully equipped and rent-free boatshop, and a generous salary to maintain the shells and assist the coaching staff.

"I still could not see my way clear to accept," he recorded, "although their offer was quite magnificent compared to what I was getting at Washington, which was only the use of the garret workshop."[1]

Delighted, and perhaps surprised, that George had declined Harvard's generous

---

1. Gordon Callow has provided an anecdote which probably best illustrates George Pocock's lifelong philosophy, which gave a low priority to the amassing of monetary wealth: "Years later, Ed Leader and Rusty Callow, then coaching at Yale and Penn respectively, knowing that during the early days Bill Boeing had at times met his payrolls with Boeing stock instead of cash, urged George to sell his shares and live more comfortably. George's reply was, 'Gentlemen, my ambition has always been to be the greatest shellbuilder in the world; and without false modesty, I believe I have attained that goal. If I were to sell the stock I fear I would lose my incentive and become a wealthy man, but a second rate artisan. I prefer to remain a first class artisan.'"

offer, Callow undertook a campaign on his friend's behalf. He arranged, through the Alumni Association, the purchase of $1,500 worth of power machinery for more efficient and less laborious production, and boatbuilding space was expanded to the ground floor area below the original shop. The additional space was needed, for Pocock shells had gained overnight fame in rowing circles, and George was well on the way to a virtual monopoly of his highly specialized trade in the United States. The eight shells ordered in the fall of 1923 following the Poughkeepsie triumph were only the beginning. Five of that first big order were for East Coast schools, including Harvard. The others went to Wisconsin, California, and Washington.

Harvard also took delivery of an English-built shell, and George was delighted to receive a clipping from the *Boston Globe* describing the trial runs of his shell and the one imported from England. As a result of the trials, the Pocock-built shell was chosen to compete in the traditional Yale-Harvard race.

Orders kept coming in, and George and his three-man crew soon formed a highly efficient working team, although none of his employees had any previous experience in boatbuilding. They had, however, worked under George's supervision at Boeing, and like most of the wartime work force, had been laid off. He was able thus to pick from the best of his former craftsmen, and they quickly mastered their new trade.

One of them in particular, a big, slow-spoken Norwegian named Hilmar Lee, was especially memorable, both as a skilled craftsman and a legendary figure among the frontiersmen of the Northwest Coast and the Klondike. George wrote of him in his memoirs:

> He was Norwegian-born, but came to the United States very early in life. After working on offshore fishing boats in Alaska, he joined with a partner in buying a boat of their own to hunt walrus and fish for salmon and halibut. Then, in 1897, he joined the Klondike gold rush. He and two partners mushed from Fort Wrangell to Dawson, packing supplies on a sled; no dogs, mind you, but drawn by hand over mountains and tundra for six hundred miles. They practically lived off the country: deer, elk, moose, and fish. He lived north of the Arctic Circle for twenty-six years.
>
> What a rugged and resourceful man he was! A good mechanic and deeply interested in his work. He was a tremendous help. I would only have to explain what should be done to a boat under construction and he would devise a better plan for doing it than I had learned. In the very early days at Boeing, department foremen were responsible for hiring their workmen. I used to place Help Wanted advertisements in the Sunday *Times*. One Monday morning this big, strong looking man came into the employment office. He was wearing a big black felt hat, similar to ones favored by Alaskans "wintering" in Seattle. Sure enough, he said he was from Nome, where he had built his own boat for freighting supplies from Nome to Kotzebue Sound. He proudly showed me a photograph of his boat. He came to work and was with me at Boeing for five years, and with me in

Pocock's crew, ca. 1924. From left to right: Malcolm MacNaught, Hilmar Lee, George Huckle, Don Huckle, Charles Turner

shell building for thirty-five years. The year before he passed on (at age ninety-two), he brought over a small plexiglass box he had made and said, "George, I want you to have this so I will know who owns it when I go." He handed me the box full of gold nuggets; specimens he had picked up from his various claims in Alaska. I looked on Hilmar as one of nature's great men . . . the rock that I leaned on.

Although the other two members of George's original crew, Charles Turner and Malcolm MacNaught, were slightly less colorful, they were intelligent and conscientious workers and the expanded Pocock boatshop was an efficient and congenial workplace.[2]

2. Stan Pocock remembers all three of his father's original building crew as "real characters." Hilmar Lee made violins as a hobby, and George always let him pick through the shop's stock of spruce to find the choicest pieces for his violin faces. When, like his boss, he lost two fingers (pushing short pieces of wood into the joiner), he was heartbroken because "I won't be able to play my fiddle any more." Eventually, he made an ingenious pair of prosthetic fingers and learned to play his beloved fiddle almost as well as before.

MacNaught, described by George as "the best boatbuilder I ever knew," later organized the highly

But continuing boat orders and increasing national recognition of his stature in the rowing world were of secondary importance to George in that landmark year of 1923. Of the most important event he wrote:

> October 11, 1923, was a red letter day in the lives of Frances and myself, for on that day a son was born, a healthy baby who was christened Stanley Richard. What a blessing. And on August 16, 1925, a daughter was born to us, Patricia May. A further blessing. Stan and Pat. They have grown big and strong, and rather than just son and daughter, they are our pals. Stan graduated in civil engineering at the University of Washington, and Pat graduated with honors from Whitman College in political science. Both are now happily married, Stan to Lois Watne and has (on this day in 1972) three children, sons Chris and Greg and daughter Susan. Pat is married to Edward Van Mason and has two children, John and Katie. A poem would be appropriate here on the blessings of children to their parents—the helpful and considerate kind, which Stan and Pat have always been:

> > Ye are better than all the ballads
> > That ever were sung or said,
> > For ye are living poems
> > And all the rest are dead.
> >   (Longfellow)

> This conveys the blessings of children to their parents. Too much cannot be said on this score. There are the other kind, unfortunately, but thank heaven we have been blessed with the kind that bring their parents great pride and happiness. Stan made his crew letter at Washington, and was a junior officer in the United States Navy during World War II. He is now head man in our boatbuilding business and doing a splendid job. Pat graduated *Cum Laude* and Phi Beta Kappa at Whitman College.

Pat shares her father's trait of understated modesty. Her letters to her parents hadn't so much as hinted at the scholastic honors she was winning, and they came as a happy surprise when they were announced at the Whitman graduation ceremonies in Walla Walla, which the Pococks, of course, attended.

"She sure hid her light under a bushel," he recalled, apparently unaware that people who knew him invariably said the same thing about him.

"But back again to 1924 and boatbuilding," George wrote in his memoirs. Babies and homebuilding were happy diversions, but his mind was never long diverted from the work that was in his very blood—the crafting of the most beautiful and functional

---

successful Colonial Furniture Company and, upon his retirement from its presidency, kept himself busy as a boatman and general helper on a volunteer basis at the Brown University boathouse.

racing shells the world had ever seen. "There was now more incentive to work hard for a growing family, there were many boats to build, and we kept up with the orders."

Once the University of Washington won the U.S. intercollegiate rowing championship, the crew quarters swarmed with budding oarsmen. The turnout was so great that many youngsters had to be cut from the squad to reduce it to a size the coaching staff could cope with.

The cuts were an aspect of rowing that never failed to sadden George. "Cutting a squad is a heartbreaking thing, because the virtues of rowing have to be denied to so many fine young men," he wrote. "It grieved me to wonder how many careers had been frustrated and weakened. It seemed to me ironic that the outstanding success of Washington crew, which we had worked so hard to attain, was resulting in the denial of rowing's benefits to many through the sheer number of applicants."

George was closely involved on a very personal basis with the generations of young oarsmen who came under his benign influence. Every coach during George's half century on the campus was wise enough to assemble each new squad to listen to the Pocock litany of praise for the spiritual and physical benefits of rowing. Delivered in his gentle, cultured voice, it was far more effective than any loud, impassioned pep talk.

It was source of great satisfaction to him that many of the crewmen snatched moments from their usually crammed schedules to come to his shop for counsel. He knew that many of them were rowing their hearts out in the little time left from demanding academic schedules. If the annual cutting of crew hopefuls was heartbreaking to him, this informal friendship with those who made it was deeply heartwarming:

"I so admired all the oarsmen, and since my shop was right at the boathouse, I got to know many of them well. I dare not name any of the hundreds of young men who came to the shop during my fifty years of service to Washington rowing, for fear I would leave some out.[3] But, generalizing, I can say there were all kindred souls, sincerely interested in painstaking work; fashioning natural material into the rowing shells of great beauty."

---

3. He did tell his friend, H. W. McCurdy, in a private conversation, that while he liked and admired all the young oarsmen, a half dozen or so retained a very special place in his heart. Among them was McCurdy's son Tom, who left the University of Washington after rowing on the freshman crew to serve as a naval officer during the Korean War. He subsequently died of a service-connected disability. George Pocock proposed to build a new shell for the university at his own expense, to be named *Tom McCurdy*. The father deeply appreciated the thought, but knowing how modest were the profits from the Pocock boatshop, he insisted on underwriting the cost of the shell, the first of several paid for by him and named for Tom.

George believed that the influence of his shells touched nonrowers, too:

> The shells we built for Eastern schools were shipped in baggage cars which were spotted on the University spur. We would carry the gleaming, newly built shells from the shop to the car and leave them outside until the holding racks were assembled inside the car. I have seen students striding along to or from classes, bowed down with worry or problems, and they would look up and see these boats and their expression would wholly change. Faces would light up with pleasure, and smiles replace strained frowns. The poet Keats wrote, "A thing of beauty is a joy forever," and I think I may say without undue immodesty that the reactions of those students proved the truth of his words.

His was the deepest satisfaction that an artist can feel—the knowledge that his masterpiece has stirred and lifted the spirit of his beholder.

In 1924, the boats still were built with much the same materials George had learned to work with as an apprentice at Eton: "We continued to use Spanish cedar for the skin of the boats, which we obtained in New York in the log, having it sawn into thick planks there, and shipped via steamer to Seattle. The shipping charge from New York to Seattle was $50 for a single log in plank form, and getting them from dockside to the boathouse cost another $50. That was a lot of money in 1924, and it worried me. I knew many schools had only very limited funds to support rowing, and I tried to keep the costs to them of racing shells as low as possible."

Eventually, George found a better and less costly wood with which to sheath his boats: western red cedar, which he henceforth referred to as "the wood eternal." George had demonstrated the virtues of Northwest cedar back in 1918, when the U.S. Navy Department conceded that the Boeing-built World War I flying boats planked with cedar were superior to the Eastern-built versions using white pine—and considerably less costly. Tradition, however, is firmly embedded in rowing and shellbuilding, and it was nearly a decade before George ventured to replace the Spanish cedar which had been the accepted material for sheathing the boats over many generations.[4]

"Nineteen twenty-seven was the first year I began using our Pacific Northwest lumber—western red cedar—for planking the boats," he wrote. "Such was the force of tradition in rowing that nothing but Spanish cedar had been considered. But I found the native red cedar to be marvelous material, ideal for the skin of racing shells; impervious to rot and light in weight. It swells and shrinks very little when

---

4. Coach Rusty Callow, who came from a family of Pacific Northwest loggers, insisted that "red cedar is only good for making shingles," and refused to have anything to do with George's "experimental" shell. Only after it was shipped to Harvard, where it proved to be a great success, did Rusty give in to the new-fangled concept.

George Pocock working on a shell, 1922–23

seasoned three years, air-dried, as we do. Its cells are complete, each containing trapped air. It is the wood eternal. Some of the first shells we built with it are still in regular use forty-five years later . . . nearly twice the useful life of the Spanish cedar boats.''

It was typical of George to be pleased that the use of this amazingly durable material "cut the cost of rowing equipment in half." This would promote the sport he loved, and for him that was the important thing. "Built-in obsolescence" was not a part of George's business philosophy.

It was also typical that he found religious significance and increased feeling for the nurturing earth in handling, shaping, and examining the fragrant wood from the giant cedars of the Northwest.

"These giants of the forest are something to behold," he wrote. "Some have been growing for a thousand years, and each tree contains its own story of the centuries long struggle for survival. Looking at the annular rings of the wood, you can tell what seasons they have been through. In some drought years they almost perished, as the growth is barely perceptible. In others, the growth was far greater. The color also varies, which I attribute to the roots getting into soil strata of different mineral content. One cannot work in wood, and study the different species, without becoming conscious of the works of the Almighty and appreciating more the words of the poet, Joyce Kilmer: 'Only God can make a tree.' "

George was particularly pleased when, a few years later, he received a letter from South America, the native land of the Spanish cedar which had for so many years been used in shellbuilding. It was an order for an eight-oared shell specifying the use of *Cedro N. Americano.*

The western red cedar shells were dubbed "banana boats" in rowing circles. The term was not derisive, for they proved to be faster as well as far more durable than the earlier ones, as George explained:

> The name banana came from the fact that the western red cedar boats had an unusual amount of camber, which curved them like a banana. This feature was not built into them. As in the past, they were built on an I-beam which was perfectly straight. The camber appears after they are built and when they are being used for their intended purpose, carrying a crew on water, and is caused by a strange characteristic of this wood. While it shrinks or swells very little *across* the grain, lengthwise it will swell or extend as much as an inch in the sixty-foot length of an eight-oared shell. During construction, the cedar skin or planking is attached to the framework in a very dry condition, therefore its shortest natural state. When completed and in use, the woodwork naturally takes in some moisture and the cedar wants to swell lengthwise, but the framework will not let it. So compression builds in the skin and the ends of the shell come up, hence your "banana boat." We like it, because when you have that compression in the shell, it makes it very lively to row.

Rudyard Kipling's fictional shipping tycoon, Sir Anthony Gloster, attributed his success to "keeping my light so shining, a little in front o' the next." George was far too modest a man to quote those lines, fond as he was of poetry, but they were certainly applicable to his success and eventual almost total domination of his chosen line of work.[5] So was Sir Anthony's appraisal of his competitors: "They copied all they could follow, but they couldn't copy my mind, and I left 'em swearing and

5. In 1952, sports editor Eugene H. Russell of the *Seattle Times* wrote: "George Pocock, master builder of college rowing shells . . . has a one-man monopoly in the rowing-craft industry but is unable to supply the demand. As a consequence, Congress recently passed special legislation lifting import duties on racing shells of foreign makers to provide equipment for training for the Olympic Games."

In the old boathouse, ca. 1940s (Life Magazine *photo*)

stealing a year and a half behind." George was not a "cussing man," but he must have been sorely tempted when the botched efforts of his competitors resulted in the banana boat design in general being viewed with suspicion in some quarters.

"Our banana boats," he recalled, "being very successful, were copied by other builders who were ignorant of the qualities and virtues of the western red cedar, and constructed them of plywood or mahogany or Spanish cedar. These materials, not being able to swell or extend lengthwise, could not put compression in the boat as ours had. These copies were dead, no life, no spring on the catch of the oars. They might just as well have been constructed of metal! So ignorance of the qualities of our western red cedar by the builders of those fake copies gave the banana boats a bad name."

Coach Rusty Callow had no doubts about the genuine article. In 1928 he was quoted in the *New York Times* as saying he believed the Poughkeepsie varsity race that year would be rowed in record time:

> Callow declares that the shells now being used, not only by Washington, but by California, Navy and Pennsylvania, are the fastest boats that have even been used in the Poughkeepsie race. The shells in question were built this year by George Pocock of western red cedar, a wood that had never been used before in the construction of the college boats. Pocock, an international authority on the construction of racing shells, has been experimenting for years with various woods in an effort to produce faster boats.
>
> Pocock, learning that the Indians of the Pacific Coast many years ago had used the local red cedar in the construction of their war canoes, some of which still exist, decided to experiment with the western cedar and found that it made a lighter and stronger shell, in his opinion, than the Spanish cedar previously used.
>
> The shell built for Washington was named the *Totem*. It is 60 feet in length, 23 1/2 inches beam, and weighs approximately 270 pounds. Coach Callow is so enthusiastic about the new boats that he thinks the record will be clipped.

George was reluctant to talk of "fast shells." Only the crews who manned them made them fast or slow. He expressed his opinion this way: "I cannot help saying right here, not having publicly or in advertisements boosted our boats, which gives me a right to say it—whenever a foreign boat wins a race or foreign oars are used, the makers crow about it from the rooftops as though the boat won the race and *not the crew*. We have always revered *the crew*. They and they alone are responsible. We try to give them a boat that will do them justice. If the boats won the races, then the makers should get the cups and medals. In the reporting of speedboat or sailing races, all the credit is given to the winning drivers or skippers. You rarely hear of who made the hulls or engines. Such should be the case in crew racing."

However, he conceded that a top-flight boat certainly didn't do a top-flight oarsman any harm:

Legendary British sculling champion Joe Burk setting a new record in the Diamond Sculls at Henley, in a Pocock-built shell (photo by George Bushell)

Some of the best correspondence I had on this subject was with Joe Burk who, after graduation from the University of Pennsylvania where he rowed four years under Rusty Callow, took up sculling in a single shell with the object of competing in the Diamond Sculls at Henley. I built him a single, planked with western red cedar, which proved a little too small. We built him a slightly larger one. While training, Joe never stopped for rough water. He would keep going with waves sweeping over the shell and hitting him on the back.

For his second year of sculling, I built him a third single, which weighed 29 1/2 pounds complete with rigging. Joe weighed 190 pounds. This one, as usual, came up at the ends from compression of the cedar after it had been used a few weeks. He took it to Henley in 1938 and won the coveted Diamond Sculls in record time, knocking ten seconds off the previous record made in 1908. An ultra-conservative opinion might be that this did not prove the boat was any faster, but it proved there was nothing wrong with it at least.

8

Olympic Gold

A L ULBRICKSON, the only coach to take a University of Washington eight-oared shell to the Olympic Games and win the Gold, was neither a verbose nor an emotional man. "Al did not wear his sentiments on his sleeve, but kept all his thoughts as to the qualities of the men under his charge to himself," George wrote. "He had them all guessing." (When Ulbrickson did have doubts about an oarsman, he usually had George go out in the coaching launch with him to judge the performance. For years, it was axiomatic among Washington crews that "when you see George Pocock out in the launch with Al there's probably going to be a change in the lineup.")

Fascinated by his apparent total lack of emotion, whether winning or losing, Eastern sports writers dubbed Ulbrickson "the Dour Dane." Royal Brougham, sports editor of the *Seattle Post-Intelligencer,* called him "the Dead Pan Kid." He wrote with a degree of awe of Al's performance when his crew came from behind to win the 1936 Poughkeepsie Regatta:

> New York has discovered the Dead Pan Kid, and New York can't get over it. "Watch this fellow Ulbrickson," was this writer's tip to the carload of scribes who went down to Po'keepsie to see the boat races. They stole a glance at the Man With the Stone Face at the very moment when his flying Washington crew was riding to its national championship. Honestly, he never as much as moved a muscle. "The guy has ice water in his veins," commented Joe Williams of the *World-Telegram.* "What a poker player that fellow would make!" said Bob Kelley of the *Times.*
>
> Get the picture—For ten years Ulbrickson had dreamed of that moment when his

varsity boat would go streaking past the finish line in first place in the greatest of all crew races. A few minutes previous the finest crew he had ever coached seemed beaten beyond all doubt.

When the tide of fortune suddenly changed, Tom Bolles pounded a stranger with his hat. The dignified George Pocock whooped in a manner which would have been deemed quite unethical in jolly old England, where the boatbuilder gained his training. George Varnell was eating the stub of his $5 press car ticket and the entire train was mad with excitement.

Al Ulbrickson's sphinx-like face never as much as quivered. Not a sound came from his lips.

The Dead Pan Kid simply slumped down in his seat with just a trace of a smile on his face as he watched with cold gray eyes the triumph of the crew created with his own hands, and heard the roar of acclaim which echoed from shore to shore.

George, who had built nineteen of the twenty-three shells which raced on the Hudson that year, also recalled Ulbrickson's unorthodox reaction to his greatest day of triumph: "At that 1936 Poughkeepsie race, his crew was dead last until the last mile, when they began overhauling every other crew one by one, took the lead, and won quite comfortably. Coming back to the boathouse after their triumph, Al was following his crew in his launch, still coaching them. Finally they were doing exactly what he wanted. 'Now that's it!' he yelled through his megaphone. 'Why didn't you row like that in the race?' One would have thought they had just lost the race instead of winning it spectacularly."

Only once in their years of association could George recall the Dour Dane showing even a trace of emotion. That was after his Husky crew defeated an outstanding Pennsylvania crew at the Olympic finals in Princeton, New Jersey: "Al was as unemotional as ever during the race in which his crew won the right to represent the United States at the Olympic Games in Berlin. Some time after the finish, he and I were walking back to the Princeton Inn. Suddenly he stopped, held out his hand and said, 'Thanks, George, for your help.' Coming from Al, that was the equivalent of fireworks and a brass band."

The Washington crewmen, as America's representatives at the Berlin Olympics, had achieved immediate VIP status. There was a week's delay between their victory at Princeton and the sailing of the United States Line's steamship *Manhattan,* upon which they would make the voyage from New York to Hamburg, and they were invited to be guests of the New York Athletic Club at its rowing quarters on Travers Island, Pelham Manor. It was an idyllic period of sunning, swimming, and relaxation after the intense competition of the past few months. George, as usual, did less relaxing than the others, as he explained in his account of the final preparations and the subsequent experiences of the Washington oarsmen in Hitler's Germany:

The 1936 University of Washington crew in their Olympic sweat clothes. From left to right: Roger Morris, bow; Charles Day; Gordon B. Adam; John G. White; James B. McMillin; George E. Hunt; Joseph Rantz; Donald B. Hume, stroke; Robert G. Moch, coxswain, kneeling

I prepared the eight-oared shell at the club boathouse, sandpapering it down, and re-varnishing it. The result was a gleaming, beautiful boat. Charles Innes, the club boatman, helped secure it on their truck, and drove from Pelham Manor through the heart of New York City to the North River pier where the *Manhattan* was moored. It appeared at first that loading the *Husky Clipper* aboard the liner would be impossible unless we got it on a scow on the outboard side, where it could be lifted by slings. Inboard were the company offices, customs shed, and passenger entrances, with insufficient space to maneuver a sixty-two-foot shell around the corners. Finally someone spotted a baggage shoot slanting down from the dock to street level where we were. It went up at about a sixty-degree angle without obstructions, so up we struggled, holding the shell at arms length. We were all in our street clothes, and it was a hot summer day. We did a great deal of sweating, but once up on the dock it was no problem to get the shell up on the boat deck, well out of harm's way.

The 1936 Olympic crew forty years later, Al Ulbrickson (second from right) filling in for Charles Day
(*photo by Bruce Terami*)

We arrived in Hamburg after slowly steaming up the Elbe River on a beautiful July evening, running aground once and waiting for the tide to lift us off. Smiling crowds lined the river banks shouting a welcome. After debarking at Hamburg, we were taken by buses to the *Rathaus,* or city hall, where the *Oberburgermeister* welcomed us, and toasts were proposed in sherry wine.

The Hitler Youth movement was flourishing, and those uniformed youngsters something to behold: straight as ramrods, blooming cheeks, close-cropped hair and bare, tanned arms and legs. The picture of health and dedication. These boys lined the great staircase as the United States Olympic team went up to the huge reception hall. Some of our lightweight boxers tried to pick fights with them along the way, but without success. Their discipline and training was such that, if they took a blow that knocked them out of line, they immediately stepped back and stood at rigid attention, obeying their orders as a guard of honor. I am sure that if their orders had been "Meet force with force," they would have struck back. They were not soldiers or policemen (although we were to learn later that they were being trained and indoctrinated for world conquest), and I thought the actions of the American boxers were thoughtless at the very least. One does not as a rule try to pick a fight with one's hosts and, like it or not, the Germans were our hosts.

From Hamburg, we journeyed by tram to Berlin, where most of the American athletes were deposited at the Olympic Village. Our oarsmen went by bus to Koepenik, a short distance from Grunaw, where the rowing events were to be held, and quartered in a police school. Our first and deepest impression of the country was the total patriotic hold Hitler had over the people. Red and white flags bearing the Nazi hooked cross were everywhere, as were uniforms of all kinds. Even the street sweepers and garbage collectors were smartly uniformed. Every telephone conversation, we noted, started and ended with "Heil Hitler."

The other competing oarsmen from the various nations were scattered around Koepenik and Grunau. The Australians—an eight-oared crew only—had already been there for several weeks. They were from the Sydney Police Rowing Club, and had stopped off first in England to row in the Royal Henley Regatta and the Grand Challenge Cup, but were barred from competition because, under the Henley Regatta rules of that time, they were classed as "professionals." Things are slow to change in England, and the event had originated for young men of sedentary occupation, the thought being that laborers, carpenters, bricklayers, and others who made their living by their strength as well as their minds were physically stronger and would thus provide unfair competition. Policemen, it appeared, were placed in that category. The rules have since been changed so that those of any occupation, from stevedores to steeplejacks and everything in between, are eligible to compete.

Twice a day the Husky crew, along with most of the other oarsmen, worked out on the water at Grunau. It didn't take us long to realize we were competing against governments. Hitler's Germany and Mussolini's Italy in particular provided total financial support to their Olympic athletes. They had the finest of equipment. In contrast the American shells, other than the *Husky Clipper,* were very old and, I thought, in disgraceful condition. There were six of the smaller boats—fours, doubles, and singles—and they were certainly the worst in use by any country.

Lawrence Terry, coach of the Harvard four with coxswain, had a highly unusual problem with his boat. He and I usually walked down to the boathouse together, but on one morning I was delayed and he got there some time before I did. When I arrived he said, "Thank heaven you're here!" He was in a terrible dither. His shell was on horses, bottom up, and all the varnish was peeling off. I asked, "What on earth have you put on it, Lawrence?" He pointed to one of two five-gallon cans brought from Seattle for use by the Washington crew. One contained sperm whale oil for putting a racing bottom on the boat; the other disinfectant for the oar handles to ward off any infection the boys might get on their blistered hands. Lawrence had applied our disinfectant to the bottom of his boat! "What shall we do?" he murmured. "Well, let's sharpen some wood scraps and get to work scraping all that loose varnish off." This we did, and then thoroughly sandpapered the bottom and applied a coat of paraffin wax to keep the water out. It was a sort of hit-or-miss job, but the boat was usable again. I thought I might cheer Lawrence up with a mild joke, and said, "Well, at least you will have the most sanitary boat in the race."

I am sorry to say that Lawrence didn't seem to appreciate my attempt at humor.

The German oarsmen were very good on the water, but ashore they tended toward arrogance, or so it seemed to our boys. The various crews all dined (and dined so well that Al had to issue strict limitations on intake) in the same building. It was customary for the various rowing squads to sing songs after dinner, usually in languages we didn't understand. One evening the Germans were in fine voice, but apparently glared at the Americans on the chorus. Our boys came to the conclusion that the words might be insulting to them, or to the Stars and Stripes, and strode over to the Germans' table with doubled fists and orders to shut up.[1] There were signs of a possible free-for-all fight, but nothing came of it. Possibly because the Aussies were showing signs of joining forces with the Yanks as a means of relieving their ennui and their frustration at having been barred from the Thames at Henley. Of course none of us really knew what was happening in pre-war Nazi Germany, but I guess we sensed that the course it was taking boded no good for the rest of the world. Americans just don't take kindly to dictatorships, especially our young men who were getting the feeling that all those Germans wearing their military and paramilitary uniforms so enthusiastically might soon force them to do the same—with much less enthusiasm. The problem surfaced again the day before the races, when all the oarsmen piled into buses to participate in the Parade of Nations at the Reichs Sports Stadium in Berlin.

At the stadium, we were all gathered in the backfield adjacent to the pavilion to await the arrival of Chancellor Adolph Hitler. He finally did, stepping out of his black Mercedes so close that I could have touched him. He marched on foot with his SS

1. George's recollection of this incident appears to have been in error. Bob Moch, coxswain of the Husky Olympic crew, said the German crews did not share the dining room with the Americans, and that it was the Yugoslavs who sang that night.

guards into the stadium, where 120,000 of his people waited. When they caught sight of him, they leaped to attention as one, arms raised in the Nazi salute and maintaining a steady screaming of *"Seig Heil."* I have never heard such blood-curdling, spine-tingling, frantic screaming in all my life. It was obvious that he literally had the German people in the palm of his hand. We could see then how this strange little man with the Charlie Chaplin mustache might well believe he could conquer the world with people like these. As he began his parade to the podium, I had a clear view of the fanatical gleam in his dark eyes and the kind of Satanic grin below the famous little mustache. I thought that tyrants and conquerors like Alexander and Genghis Khan probably had eyes like his.

As we paraded with the athletes of other nations, we saw that other national contingents lowered their country's flags, held their headgear in their left hands, and saluted with their right as they marched in step to the band music past the Fuhrer's reviewing stand.

Word passed through the American squad like magic. The Stars and Stripes was not lowered to the Nazi dictator, and we strolled past, deliberately out of step. We did remove our hats and hold them over our hearts as we went by, as a mark of courtesy to our host nation. It was a very small blow for freedom certainly, but it somehow made us feel a lot better.

The next morning we were back at Koepeneck for the first day of racing by the singles, doubles, and two classes of fours in elimination heats, followed by the eights. We won our heat, barely nosing out Great Britain in what was then world's record time.

The following day, in the finals, Germany won the first five events, and we got a bit weary of the crowds standing at the Hitler salute singing *two* national anthems. In the sixth race, the double sculls, Germany and Great Britain were neck-and-neck, well in the lead, coming into the last hundred meters. The British crew barely nosed out the Germans to win the Gold Medal. It was nice to hear *God Save the King* for a change. Then came the big one, the race of the six eight-oared shells which had survived the earlier heats.

Al Ulbrickson was blessed that year with an outstanding stroke oar as well as Bob Moch, one of the great coxswains in Washington's rowing history. Don Hume was not a big man, weighing about 165 pounds (the next lightest stroke in the Poughkeepsie Regatta that year had outweighed him by 18 pounds), but Don was a "natural," always giving the big men behind him plenty of time for the proper "run" between strokes. To be of championship caliber, a crew must have total confidence in each other, able to drive with abandon, confident that no one man will get the full weight of the pull. Without this confidence, the men tend to "row with the boat," meaning they will not pull faster than the boat is going. A good run between strokes is impossible under these conditions because the oarsmen have to rush up on the slide for the next stroke to attain a higher beat. The 1936 crew, with Hume at stroke, rowed with abandon, beautifully timed. Having complete confidence in one another, they would bound on the stroke with one powerful cut; then ghost forward to the next stroke with the boat running true and with hardly a perceptible slowdown. They were a classic example of eight-oared rowing at its very best, and both Al and I were confident that only Great Britain was capable of beating them.

The wind, which had been gentle and in the crews' favor in earlier races, had veered clear around by the time the eights lined up for the start, and was blowing briskly against them. A verbal starting signal was used, and our coxswain, Bob Moch, could not hear it. That resulted in a slow start, but that didn't phase him or the rest of the crew. Al and I, standing on a roof near the finish line, could see the *Husky Clipper* moving up fast. It was soon obvious that there were only three boats still in the money, ours and two we couldn't at first identify, all bunched up together, Washington on the far side. We assumed that one must be the British, but as they drew closer we saw that it was Germany and Italy, the two government-financed crews.

The last hundred meters, the huge crowd in the grandstands began chanting for Germany, their words in time with the German crew's stroke: *"Deutsch-land! Deutsch-land! Deutsch-land!"* But in a final effort, Hume ran the Washington stroke up a bit and *Husky Clipper* nosed out Italy and Germany in that order. Our amateurs from the University of Washington had won the Gold Medal in the big one for the United States of America!

Following Olympic tradition, the Husky crew pulled into the dock, where a laurel wreath was placed on the coxwain's head and the crew paraded in front of the stands. Coxswain Moch squished a little as he marched, for his mates had not forgotten the old American tradition of throwing the winning coxswain overboard, to the amazement and delight of the German spectators, who were not familiar with the custom.

Royal Brougham, the *Post-Intelligencer* sports editor, had joined Al and me on the roof for the thrilling finish, and he was just as excited and pleased as we were. He headed at top speed for a telegraph office and burned up the wires with the glorious news for the home folks. That night he took us and our wives to dinner at the posh Adlon Hotel in Berlin. I don't remember what we ate, but I know what we drank. Hitler may have modernized Germany's highways, railways, and military forces, but we had yet to find decent-tasting drinking water. The Adlon, we found to our delight, served delicious, sparkling fresh water, and we couldn't get enough of it. The wine steward would come to our table wearing his golden key around his neck, and we would all say "Wasser, bitte." Finally he left a full jug on our table. It made us realize what a blessing good fresh drinking water is, especially if you are from Seattle or the state of Washington.

The next day we attended some of the closing events at the stadium, but it was an anticlimax for us. We had won the Gold, and the 1936 Olympiad was just past history to us. We wanted very badly to leave the screaming crowds of uniformed and regimented Germans, and breathe the air of freedom again.

George and Frances, and Al Ulbrickson and his wife, traveled together to England after the games. The wives had been impressed by a Sunday trip to Frederick the

The University of Washington crew, upper left, crosses the finish line at Berlin

Great's Sans Souci Palace near Berlin, but George stayed loyal to his boyhood memories of Windsor Castle. "I told the others that if they would hurry up and pack I would show them a *real* palace," he wrote.

"We duly reached London and old memories came flooding back even as the train pulled into Paddington Station. In 1904, a famous Harley Street surgeon, Sir Francis Lakin, had departed Paddington on board the royal train. King Edward VII was suffering from appendicitis, a usually fatal condition known generally in those days as 'inflamation of the bowels,' and Dr. Lakin was to operate on him at Windsor. I was at the Windsor station to see this wonderful man in whose hands the king's life rested, elegant in morning coat, striped trousers, and silk top hat, and followed by his man servant. They entered the royal coach with its postillions and outriders, and were whisked off to Windsor Castle, where Sir Francis performed the operation successfully."

George's father, old Aaron Pocock, met them at the station, and his son was saddened to see the toll the malicious years had taken upon him. He wrote in his journal:

> He was now seventy-eight years old, and looked very tired. I couldn't help thinking of all the adversities he had suffered: bankrupt in business because of his love for artistry; loss of his wife, our mother, and, four years later, the loss of his second wife; fired from his beloved job as head of the Eton College boathouse because he was far ahead of Victorian England's concept of proper human relations, and was thought to be too "easy" on the working men in his crew. Then he was employed by the London County Recreation Council, also building boats. In twenty years he would have earned a lifetime pension. He was fired after nineteen years and six months!
>
> At age seventy, he was knocked off his bicycle by an automobile. His back was broken, and the doctors said he would never walk again. He did eventually walk, but only with the aid of a cane. It was a sweet yet sad reunion after so many years.
>
> We put up at a London hotel, and as we were driving from the station in a taxi, on the left side of the street of course, we came to a sharp curve and went scooting around it at a brisk pace. Al Ulbrickson, I noticed, was white faced and white knuckled, braced for what he seemed to consider an inevitable collision. It's a frightening experience to those not accustomed to driving British style.[2]
>
> We went down to Windsor and Eton as I wanted the Ulbricksons to see Eton College and its boathouses, as well as majestic Windsor Castle. I am sure they enjoyed it. We climbed the time-worn steps to the top of the round tower, where all around us the

---

2. Possessed of an intensely inquiring mind, George Pocock was impelled to research the background and tradition of anything unusual he saw or heard about. He added the following hand-written note to his typed journal: "I might add that driving on the left hand side of the road in olden times was a necessity. People on horseback were apt to be waylaid by armed thieves even in those days, and being on the left hand side freed the rider's right or sword arm to defend himself."

spectacular view I remembered so well from my boyhood; the River Thames winding all over the green countryside as it had in the time of William the Conqueror, when it was named Winds-o'er the Countryside.

As we returned to ground level, a massive door opened in the wall and a man in working clothes said, "Would you like to see the Queen's garden?" He took us inside where we saw that the former moat had been filled in with soil and transformed into a beautiful garden. The old chap said as we were leaving, "Sir, would you have a place for a gardener at your estate in America?" All Americans were thought to be millionaires. We relieved his mind on that score, and he asked, "Would you like some seeds from the Queen's garden?" We bought the proffered packet and planted them back in Seattle upon our return. They turned out to be Dusty Millers, some of which are still growing in our considerably more modest garden.

We even went to see Mrs. Dear, who ran the Eton candy store to which we gave our custom as children. After a quarter century away, I found the customs hadn't changed much in the little town, but Frances and the Ulbricksons found them fascinating. Mrs. Dear invited us all in for "afternoon tea," a British custom as cherished as the changing of the guard at Buckingham Palace. One of the workmen who lodged at Mrs. Dear's came in for his "cuppa," and his method of drinking it was a work of art. He poured the hot tea in the saucer, and with a unique hold on the saucer and a corkscrew turn of the wrist, he had the tea gulped down in no time. I remember Al and the ladies gazing at the performance almost transfixed.

Then we took a tour through the Eton College boathouses to see the 650 boats all racked up in orderly fashion, making one realize the extent to which rowing was used for training these young Eton boys, where the song goes:

> They feather their oars
> With skill and dexterity,
> Winning each heart
> And delighting each eye.
> Chorus: Swing, swing together, etc.

After seeing the Ulbricksons off for home, my wife and I returned to Eton for another week's stay so I could renew acquaintances and old friendships, especially that of my closest boyhood chum, Jimmy Ottrey. After our first night at the Bridge House Hotel, Jimmy and his wife persuaded us to spend the rest of our stay at their house. I could remember my disappointment when Jimmy fell in love with Grace. I knew it was the beginning of the end to an inseparable friendship in which we had shared all our favorite sports—rowing, cycling, target shooting, and some cross-country running.

The first evening at the Ottreys, Grace said to me, "George, do you remember what you said to Jim when you learned we were planning to be married?" I replied, "Grace, I do not, but I was a bit heartbroken as I felt I was losing my best chum. What did I say?" Grace smiled and told me, "You said, Jim, you are a cussed fool." Having seen their obvious happiness in their marriage, and having enjoyed similar happiness in my own, I said, "Well, Grace and Jim, after twenty-five years, I apologize."

On his way back from Berlin, George Pocock rows at Eton in the single he had built for his professional sculling debut twenty-six years earlier.

The next day we went down to the college boathouse and met two of the men who were there when Dad was the manager and I was an apprentice. Almost all the boathouse crew had nicknames, and these were "Froggy" Windsor and "Bosh" Barret. Much hearty handshaking and back-slapping ensued, and Froggy said, "George, we still have your single and it's in good shape. Are you going to take it out?" I replied eagerly, "I sure will! Bosh, can you find me some rowing togs?" Bosh went into the Eight Room (the dressing, study and tea room reserved for the Eton varsity eight) and returned with a pair of shorts and a zephyr [shirt]. After changing, I shoved off into the stream for a scull up the river in the first scull I had ever built, twenty-seven years earlier, the one which helped me win the fifty pound prize money that paid my way to North America. Talk about nostalgia! I drank in every foot of the well remembered course, and memories, memories. Oh dear, oh dear, what a thrill. Frances took movies of me going by.

After that we went up to the college boatbuilding shop, where two men were building a single. One of them was Ben Logan, the son of boatbuilder who had worked there when my dad was manager. The thought passed through my mind that if dad had not lost his job, I might be there working alongside Ben, and at that point in my life I certainly wouldn't have wanted to be. The Bard again—"It's an ill wind that blows no man good."

Leaving the boathouse, we strolled down Eton High Street to the college, with me pointing out the places that had been so important to me in my early youth. There was the fire station, where Dick and I had drilled as members of the fire brigade; the school where we had received our formal education; the church where, as a child, I had suffered such torment on those awful seats. All brought more memories rushing back. At the school, I had won a cash scholarship. The winners each year had their names emblazoned on a board inside the entrance. My name was still there, and I remembered vividly how proud I had been as a child when it first appeared there. Revisiting the little church, I remembered how I had puzzled over the Scriptural admonition taught in Sunday School, "Unless you be as little children, you cannot enter the Kingdom of Heaven." I feared it meant that if I died as a child, only I would enter Paradise and I would never see my father or mother or grandparents again. The true meaning should have been explained to us—that it referred not to age, but to the thinking and receptive mind of a little child.

I was a bit disillusioned by one of the landmarks of my childhood, Layton's Restaurant on the High Street. During those school days, we had an hour for lunch and, on the way home, passed over a grating above the restaurant kitchen below. Wafting up from it came the most delectable odors—roast beef, puddings, and fruit pies. Our imaginations told us it must serve the most marvelous food in the world. There was no spare money for restaurant dining in those days.

It was with some sense of triumph and anticipation that I ushered Frances into Layton's for lunch. I soon realized that growing children must have very sharp appetites, for we found the food quite commonplace. Or perhaps it was the wisdom of nature telling us we should lessen our intake.

I roamed the town and countryside with Jim Ottrey, too, as we had done a quarter of a century before, and looking at him, I could not believe that so many years had come and gone. We took a trip to Henley with the Ottreys, and caught the river steamer back to Eton, having tea on board. These pretty little steamers ran from Oxford to London, a two day trip on the Thames; a restful voyage if ever there was one.

Taking our leave of my old friends, we journeyed to London to visit my father at Battersea. He had married again, a pleasant little woman named Em, and they had one son, Billy. Their house was a very small one, and we were fortunate enough to rent a room at a house next door owned by a widow, Mrs. Polly. She pronounced it "Po-lee," much to dad's disgust. "She's putting on airs," he grumbled.

Following their stay in London, the Pococks made a bus tour of Scotland, returning to Battersea for a final farewell to Aaron, who had been worried because he hadn't heard from them. Their trip had taken only three days. Finally, George recorded, "came the day of parting. A taxi picked us up at dad's place, and the last we ever saw of that noble and courageous man was him running along the sidewalk, pantomiming that he was going to keep up with us. On the train to Southampton, five people occupied the seats on each side of our compartment, all strangers and all very British. Not a word was spoken the whole distance. None of us had been introduced!" He continued,

> After an uneventful Atlantic crossing and a few days in New York, we returned home by train, with a side trip to Ithaca to meet the new Cornell crew coaches, Harrison (Stork) Sanford and Norman Sonju, both ex-Husky oarsmen. Incidentally, I picked up an order for two new eights from the athletic department there. By then I was itching to reach Seattle again and get to work. All this Olympic service had been gratis, and I remembered Dad had gone broke in the boatbuilding business because of too much work done without payment.
>
> What a pleasure to get home and see the children, relatives, and friends there to meet us at the station. So back to work, and plenty of it to do.

In spite of George's self admonition against too much "gratis" work, his loyalty to rowing continued to cut down on his potential profits. He consistently kept the prices of his shells as low as possible. In the mid 1930s, *Seattle Times* sports columnist George Varnell recorded that UCLA, then a comparatively new university, was attempting to institute its first rowing program. Major Goodsell, the newly appointed coach, came to the Pocock boatshop to order two shells, all the university could afford at that time. George felt two weren't enough to get the program off to a proper start, and as Varnell wrote: "When Pocock took the two shell order he wrote three instead of two. The third shell was his personal gift to rowing at UCLA. The gift of the shell probably meant the profit on the two ordered, but to Pocock that means nothing. That he is doing his part to help the sport is his reward and satisfaction.

"That's George Pocock."

9

Races 'round the World

D URING THE NEXT FOUR OLYMPIADS, in 1948, 1952, and 1956, George reverted
to unprofitable amateur status to accompany the American oarsmen as boatman and, when required, as coach.

The threat of world war which he had sensed in Nazi Germany in 1936 had become
a reality by 1940, when the next Olympiad was scheduled for Tokyo. Japan was at
war with China by then, and Hitler's seemingly invincible military forces were poised
to conquer all of Western Europe. In ancient times, a sacred truce was declared for
the games, allowing all participants to travel unmolested to the ancient Greek religious
center of Olympia. Modern warfare has no such civilized overtones, and the games
were canceled. The first post-war Olympiad was held in London, still rebuilding
after the Luftwaffe bombings, in 1948. The rowing events were held on the Thames
at Henley.

The American Olympic trials that year were held at Princeton, New Jersey, where
Ky Ebright's University of California eight won the right to represent the United
States. The University of Washington four with coxswain was the winner in its class.
Again, George went as boatman to all the American crews, and coach of the University
of Washington four, which Al Ulbrickson had turned over to him after the winning
race at Princeton. Frances accompanied him, staying with Jim and Grace Ottrey at
Eton. Much as he enjoyed being involved in his beloved sport in familiar surroundings,
George (and Ebright) found the course at Henley less than ideal for the task of getting
their crews in condition to meet the challenge of the world's finest oarsmen:

114

George Pocock lends a hand to the varsity eight at the University of Washington, 1946 (Life Magazine photo). *Visible are Grant Bishop* (stroke) *and Jim Tupper.*

Two days of trying to practice at Henley were more than enough for us. No coaching launches were allowed on the course, so we had to direct our crews from the towpath while riding bicycles! Ky tried using a tandem bike, with his manager up front to steer along the tricky towpath; Ky with his megaphone at the back. To add to the confusion, the river was jammed with so many boats that it was hard to find space to swing an oar. We agreed it was certainly coaching the hard way.

I had told Ky, crossing on the S.S. *America,* of the conditions he would probably find at Henley, and that it would be wise to train at Marlow, about eight miles down river. There is a four-mile stretch of open water there between locks with very little traffic, and we could use launches. After those two days of frustration at Henley, he was anxious to learn more about the idyllic location I had described. "OK, Ky," I said. "Let's get a launch, pile the trunks in, and the boys can row the boats down through two locks, and there will be the Marlow Rowing Club, where I am sure they will let us house the boats." I also explained that Marlow is closer to Finnemore Wood where the United States and South American oarsmen were staying.

The move was a blessing. Both the eight and the four got in some splendid conditioning rows. It would have been better had all the U.S. entries come down to Marlow, where it was quiet, and the handicap of watching other crews was eliminated. Watching other crews at work tends to draw oarsmen into some points of the others' style. It is best, if possible, to keep them apart.

Back at Henley for the actual racing, our four survived the preliminary heats, but had a narrow squeak against France. My racing plan has always been, whether rowing my own single or advising a crew, "Know your own capabilities and *row your own race.*" Row each 500 meters about the same, but be sure you are rowed out at the finish. Keep your eyes in the boat; let your coxswain be your eyes. I have seen close races lost when one crew member failed to heed that advice and lost the stroke because his mind wasn't focused entirely on his rowing.

In the semifinal race with the French four, the crew asked if they could go off with the lead. In the two preliminary races they had started at a lowered stroke, and only gained the lead in the last 500 meters. I said, "Yes, but I hope you won't be sorry."

So they started off at a very high stroke, but were unable to get out in front. They were obviously well off their pace, but finally settled down to their usual beat, began to gain steadily, and ended up the winner. I knew by the times they had made previously that both Denmark and Holland were better than France, and they were the two crews we had to meet in the final race for the Gold. The day after the semifinals was a Sunday and there was no racing. I wanted to make good use of that time. The American four had lost some of their technique in the excitement of two days of highly competitive racing. They had lost the essential art of keeping a strong, clean run on the boat between strokes.

Sunday afternoon we went out above the bridge where I could coach from a launch, and went to work. We went up and down the river time after time, but we just weren't getting it. A coach has to be a dictator at times, and I said, "We are not going in until we get that run between strokes." A good run is attained by hanging on to, or "squeezing" the finish, at the same time returning to at least an upright position, so that the weight is out of the bow via the squeeze of the blade in the water. The wrong way is finishing with the oar out of the water and the body weight of the crew in the bow.

At last it seemed they were beginning to regain the hang of it, and just as dusk was setting in, they made a beautiful run, the boat fairly ghosting along between strokes.

"That's it! That's it for tomorrow. Let's go in!"

Monday's final race was tough and close, but it was a clear-cut victory for the University of Washington four in the shell *Clipper Too,* which I had built twelve years earlier.

The presentation of the Olympic Gold Medals is an impressive ceremony, with our five boys at attention on the podium, eyes on Old Glory rising to the masthead while the military band played the Star Spangled Banner. It tends to bring a lump to one's throat, along with the reflection that all the hard work on everybody's part had been well worthwhile. The five young men who won the Gold for the United States on the Thames in 1948 were Warren Westland, stroke; Bob Martin, number 3; Bob Will,

The University of Washington's unbeaten four with coxswain line up at Henley in 1948 to receive the Olympic Gold. From left to right: Allen Morgan, coxswain; Warren De Haven Westland, stroke; Robert D. Martin; Robert J. Will; Gordon S. Giovanelli

number 2; Gordon Giovanelli, bow; and Allen Morgan, coxswain. They deserve to be remembered, for the four-oared race with cox is the most hotly contested rowing event in Europe, and to this day, that was the only American four to have won the Gold in the Olympic Games.

The Danish crew came in a very close second in that race, and if their coach, Ernie Barry, who was ex-sculling champion of the world, had been with them, it might have been a different story. Barry had taken them to the European championship two years in a row, but wasn't allowed at Henley, because he wasn't a citizen of Denmark as required under Olympic rules. He had sent me a letter in which he wrote "Look out George, for the Danish crew. They are *nippy*."

That was a great year for American crews at the Olympics, the California varsity eight under Ky Ebright winning the Gold in the same Olympics. It is noteworthy that ours were the only two crews to escape the crowded river at Henley and do our training on the quiet waters at Marlow. Another plus was the great fellowship which sprang up between our two crews from two different and competing universities from different states and with different coaches.

The 1952 Olympics were held at Helsinki, Finland, and George had the responsibility of building seven shells for all the American oarsmen who were competing.

These consisted of an eight, four-oared with coxswain, four without cox, pair-oared with cox, pair-oared without cox, a double sculling shell, and a single sculling shell, along with the necessary oars and sculling oars. These were built and crated, and loaded aboard the Swedish cargo liner M.V. *Seattle* of the Johnson Line. The captain was most cooperative, agreeing to stow the shells on the boat deck, well out of harm's way. The ship's first port of call in Finland was Kotka, almost a hundred miles up the Gulf of Finland from Helsinki, where no stop was scheduled. The captain was apologetic, but explained that he would have to receive orders from company headquarters in Malmo to alter the schedule. I had met the man in charge of the Swedish rowing contingent at the 1948 Olympics, Gunnar Nitzell. I sent off an air mail letter to him, asking him to intervene with the ship's owners to allow the *Seattle* to put in at Helsinki to offload the shells for the American Olympic rowing team. Word came back, almost by return mail, that permission was granted.

While supervising the stowing of the shells aboard ship, George had been much impressed by the luxurious accommodations for the twelve passengers carried on the Johnson Line cargo ships. Frances agreed that it would be a wonderful way to travel to Helsinki. The *Seattle*'s sister ship, *Golden Gate,* was scheduled to sail from Seattle on May 23. The ships made leisurely voyages by way of various West Coast ports, the Panama Canal and the Netherland West Indies, Central American ports and Curacao, but there would be enough time to disembark at Gotenburg and arrive in Helsinki a few days before the first scheduled rowing events on July 19.

Although the Johnson Line ships, noted for their passenger amenities, friendly crews, and marvelous food, were always booked far ahead, George, having sent the American Olympic shells to Finland by one of the company's vessels, qualified as a "shipper," a class beloved of the owners of cargo liners. As such, he and Frances "bumped" some unfortunate nonshipper, and were even allowed to board the *Golden Gate* at Seattle, although ordinary passengers had to travel overland to the ship's namesake city, San Francisco.

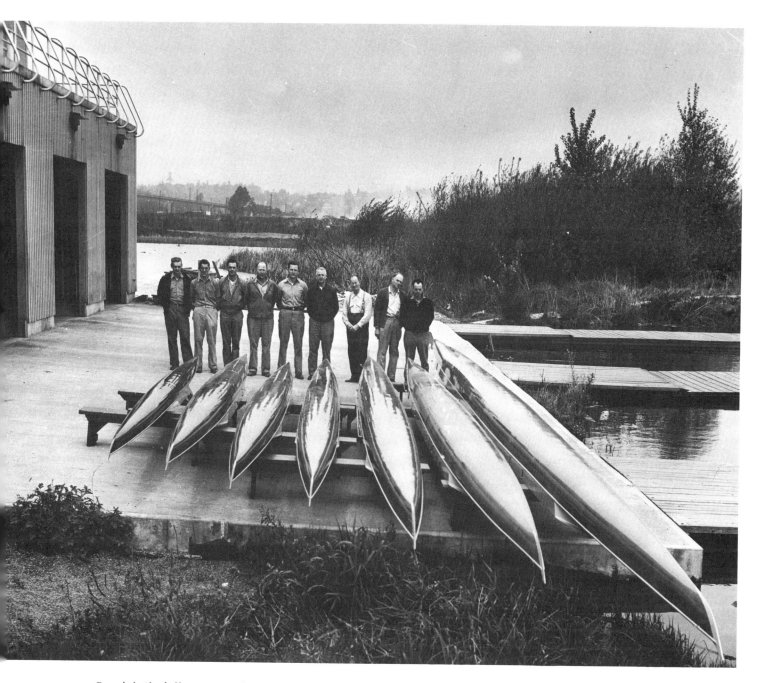

Pocock-built shells awaiting shipment to Helsinki, Finland, for use by U.S. Olympic crews, 1952

As usual, George was able to find an analogy in the lines of the Immortal Bard: "Kissing goes by favor."

Blessed by beautiful weather and congenial fellow passengers, the voyage was a

George and Frances Pocock leave for Helsinki.

month-long delight. George noted that when he and Frances debarked they were enjoying "nerves like a slowly flowing river." The ship's departure from Seattle had been delayed several days, and George had decided he should be in Helsinki well before the American crews arrived on July 12. Accordingly, they left the ship at

Antwerp, taking a train to Brussels where, after a two-day stay, they flew to Goteburg, where they were met at the terminal by Gunnar Nitzell, who had contacted the airline for the passenger list and had already made arrangements for the Pococks' voyage across Sweden by canal boat to Stockholm.

The three-day canal trip across Sweden was another idyllic experience. The perfect summer weather persisted, and the boat traversed a lovely rural countryside, sometimes with fat cows grazing almost within reach alongside. There were frequent stops at the sixty-five locks along the route as the canal boat climbed to three hundred feet above sea level, sometimes through solid rock excavations, sometimes bisecting country roads with hand-operated sliding bridges.

From Stockholm, it was a short air hop to Helsinki, where George headed at once for the boathouses and the boats. Finding that they had all survived the voyage from Seattle very well, he set to work getting the riggers on, the slides oiled, and the oars greased. Everything was, even by his perfectionist standards, "all shipshape and Bristol fashion" for the arrival of the American oarsmen. He was surprised, and a bit flattered no doubt, by the attention the Pocock-built American shells received from the Europeans:

> The foreign builders who were there set up their drawing boards and copied the lines of our boats. Russia, for the first time, had a full squad of oarsmen there, with a German coach and using German-built shells. Unlike the Germans and Italians, who didn't ask permission to copy our boats, the Russians did, via their coach, much to their credit. The Russian athletes were also very friendly with our boys, although they could only communicate with smiles and handshakes. Finally one of them came over to our tent and asked if any of us "Sprechen die Deutsch." One did, and the two joined in animated conversation in German. Afterward the gang gathered around our German-speaking colleague asking, "What did he say? What did he say?"
>
> The reply was, "He said that what goes on between our political leaders in Moscow and Washington has nothing to do with your men or our men. We are friends. We are all *oarsmen*."
>
> The Cold War was escalating, but the Olympic tradition and ideals were still working, bringing these young Russian and American athletes together as friends and fellow oarsmen, members of a worldwide fraternity that reaches beyond politics and national frontiers.

The American crews were somewhat amused by the Soviet style of rowing, describing almost a full circle with their oar blades—"like a windmill"—according to George. He felt that the Navy crew, coached by his old friend Rusty Callow, would have little trouble with them in the eight-oared competition, and they didn't. It was Navy all the way for the Gold, but the Soviets, despite their unorthodox stroke, took the

University of Washington four-oared crew with coxswain represented the United States at the 1952 Olympics, winning the Bronze Medal behind Czechoslovakia and Switzerland. From left to right: Fil Leanderson; Dick Wahlstrom; Al Ulbrickson, Jr.; Carl Lovsted; Al Rossi, coxswain

Silver in their first Olympic try. Australia, beginning to emerge as a rowing power, claimed the Bronze. Washington's cox and four also won a Bronze medal.

George was not impressed with the other American crews, except for the two-oared shell without coxswain. He felt it had a good chance to claim another Gold medal for the United States, and that proved to be the case. His prediction wasn't based on a hunch, but on a very simple theory which he explained this way:

> I must state my reason for picking the pair without cox as winners. They had learned to row *without a rudder*. My Dad had always said that if a pair could learn to row without a rudder, they would be at least two lengths faster than a boat with a rudder over a 2,000-meter course. Chuck Logg, crew coach at Rutgers and coach of this pair,

was the first I know of to have taken this advice. Ordinarily the bow man steers, with the rudder lines attached to his stretcher boot. If the stroke man is the stronger, the bow man simply sets the rudder against him. Even if they pull evenly, the rudder causes a drag and will oscillate a little, stopping the way a bit; enough to lose a hotly contested race.

The bow man of the Rutgers pair was the coach's son, Chuck Logg, Jr., a senior and a top-flight oarsman. The stroke was Tom Price, a husky freshman. Together they could row a course as straight as if their shell were on rails. I asked young Chuck Logg if he had any problems pulling even with Tom. "Oh," he said, "I have no trouble staying with him the first thousand meters, but the last thousand I have to give it absolutely everything I've got to keep us on a straight course." And there you have it, the logic of my Dad's conviction. If the shell had been fitted with a rudder, it would have been only human nature to use it against Tom toward the end of the race, and they would not have won. Having no rudder places an equal burden on both men and requires them to give everything they've got, which is what wins races.

Only two other coxless pairs competing in subsequent Olympic Games have taken this advice, and they both won the Gold Medals, constituting the only three American crews to take the top honors in this event. Those who followed the lead of Logg and Price were Hecht and Fifer in 1956 at Melbourne, and Jackson and Hungerford at Tokyo in 1964. We send this bit of advice along with every coxless pair we ship to anyone, but few indeed have heeded it. Not that that is unusual. We have imparted equally sound advice on other phases and classes of competitive rowing, with equally few listeners. Perhaps I should have added a sledge hammer to my shop equipment. To drive my good advice home.

Despite his early association with pioneers of the aircraft industry and his stint at Boeing in its early years, George never became enthusiastic about air travel. He and Frances returned home via Pan American Airlines, a flight which he described as "a trying trip of 24 hours," with the result that "we were so tired that we slept like logs in noisy New York; the first time ever." The flight home was a great deal quicker than the relaxing cruise aboard the *Golden Gate,* but the Pococks obviously didn't enjoy it nearly as much.

Between the 1952 and 1956 Olympic Games, the firm of George Pocock Racing Shells, with a crew of a dozen craftsmen, including George's son Stan, was humming with activity. The reputation of those functionally beautiful Pocock shells had spread to rowing circles everywhere. The little company had a virtual monopoly in the United

This University of Washington varsity crew came in second at Marietta in 1951 (photo by James Sneddon).

States, and even Oxford University in England broke a tradition of more than a century when it had a Pocock-designed eight built for its ancient rivalry with Cambridge.

The regular routine of the boatshop was frequently broken by panic calls from coaches and crews when emergencies arose involving boats and equipment. It was well known that George was the best man available to solve their problems, and that he simply was unable to resist dropping everything to rush to the aid of oarsmen who, after months of arduous training, might face elimination from final competition by loss or damage to their shell. One such crisis developed north of the border in British Columbia in 1954:

This was another notable year in rowing, as the British Empire Games were to be held in Vancouver, B.C. (I think they are called the Commonwealth Games now, as there is no Empire.) The University of British Columbia, combined with the Vancouver Rowing Club, had a crew training for the eight-oared event. We built them a new shell named the *Victor Spencer,* who I believe was the donor. Frank Read was the coach and he was whipping together a fine crew. The trials to decide what crew would represent Canada were to be held at St. Catherines, Ontario. Departure for this event was two days away, and the last time trial at Vancouver was under way. Read and others in the coaching launch were amazed at the time the British Columbia crew was making, their eyes glued to their stopwatches. The coxswain was looking incredulously at the shoreline flashing by. No one saw the big low-lying log right in the path of the speeding shell when, CRASH! The boat rode right up on it with a sickening, splintering noise. One of the boys in the shell who had worked in the woods said it sounded like a falling tree crashing to the ground and smashing off branches of surrounding trees as it fell. It had been an early morning workout, and at seven that same morning my telephone rang at home. It was Frank Read, and as soon as I heard his voice I said, "Frank, you have busted your boat!" I seemed to feel it in my bones. "Yes," he said, "we ran over a log. Can you come up and get us out of trouble? We have to leave for St. Catherines day after tomorrow."

I told him Stan and I would get there as soon as possible, but it would be late; probably about ten o'clock that night. In the meantime, I told him to get the damaged shell up to the social hall, where we would have heat and good lighting. Stan and I had some work to finish before we could get away, but by five o'clock in the evening we had the station wagon loaded with all the paraphernalia we felt we would need, and headed north. We stopped at Bellingham for dinner and telephoned Frank Read to let him know we were well on our way.

But when we stopped at Blaine for Canadian Customs inspection, the inspector peered into the jampacked rear of our station wagon, shook his head, and informed us, "You will have to make an exact inventory of all the stuff you have in there and we'll have to check it again when you return." We explained that this was an emergency situation; that the University of British Columbia was competing in the Commonwealth Trials in the eight-oared event, that they had smashed their boat that very morning, and that we had dropped everything to come up and get them out of trouble. The Customs man must have been a UBC fan, for he grinned and said, "OK, go ahead. And good luck," waving us on.

We arrived at the clubhouse right on schedule, the boat was up in the social hall under the lights and looking very sad, as were the oarsmen, who were sitting around it like mourners at a funeral. Stan and I examined the smashed shell very closely and decided we could have it ready by about noon the next day. We went to work immediately and kept at it until one o'clock in the morning. After some four hours' sleep at Frank Read's home, we returned at six, and by noon the boat was ready. We gave it a good flowing coat of varnish, and by the following morning it was in its crate and loaded on the train for St. Catherines.

The crew won the right to represent Canada at the Games against a fleet of Eastern Canada boats, much to the surprise of the Easterners, and went on to win the finals, rowing against Great Britain.

Nor was that the only Pocock rescue mission for participants in the Canadian regatta. Officials in Vancouver telephoned the boat shop in Seattle to explain that the New Zealand four with coxswain was without a shell, theirs having been held up by a waterfront strike in Honolulu. George had a brand new one in the shop, and told the New Zealanders to come and get it. William Stevenson, a long time champion single sculler and doubles co-champion who was in charge of the New Zealand oarsmen, hired a truck and picked it up. A couple of weeks later it was returned, with a request for a billing. George, of course, charged nothing for its use. "Simply a courtesy of American rowing to our brother oarsmen from New Zealand," he explained. Besides, he felt himself well rewarded with the continuing friendship of Stevenson (later Sir William), whom he described as "the most self-effacing, hard-working, charitable man I have ever known." It was a friendship which would be most pleasantly renewed following the 1956 Olympiad held at Melbourne, Australia.

The oarsmen of the British Commonwealth Regatta showed their respect and affection for George by asking him to be the speaker at the banquet to be held at Vancouver for all the participating crews. George always showed a modest reluctance to accept such invitations, insisting there must be others more qualified than he, but when pressed, he always gave in.

In this case he hedged his bets, as he explained in his memoirs:

I tried to chicken out of it, but compromised, and said I would providing Canada won the eights. They did, so I had to go. It was a congenial gathering, and the man who introduced me was Reggie Woodward, an oldtimer up there in club rowing. He made a long, flowery introduction, after which I thanked him, but also said, "Reggie, you have left yourself wide open to my favorite introduction story. The chairman, the story goes, was waving his gavel around as he introduced the speaker, and accidentally konked him on the head, knocking him out. Failing to notice what he had done, he kept on lauding the virtues of the impending speaker until the latter finally came to. He gasped out, "Hit me again. I can still hear you."

My talk went all right after the laughter had died down. It centered around what I had learned in Finland during the 1952 Olympic Games, particularly what I had learned from the remarkable, courageous people of that tiny country. I had asked one man in Helsinki if the Finns weren't worried about being in the shadow of the totalitarian and repressive Soviet Union. After putting up a defense that amazed the world, little Finland had finally fallen to the Red army early in World War II, the Soviets imposing reparations which almost bankrupted the conquered nation. But Finland met them and remained a happy, hopeful people, and by 1952 had recovered sufficiently to stage a most successful Olympiad—a country with a total population of only about four million people. "Well!," my Finnish friend explained, "we all have *Siesu*." "What on earth is *Siesu*?" I asked. He replied, "It is a Finnish word that means fortitude, courage, a whole soul that looks always on the pleasant side; a word that sums up all the virtues that make up a successful human being."

The 1956 Olympiad was held in Melbourne, and George was named boatman for the United States rowing team, in addition to building the seven shells it would use in world competition. Under the direction of Clifford "Tip" Goes, chairman of the Olympic Rowing Committee, the completed boats were stowed aboard an Australia Direct Line steamship for delivery at Sydney. With happy memories of their 1952 voyage to Helsinki by cargo liner, and with knowledge of the advantages of being a "shipper," George and Frances obtained passage on a later sailing of the Australia Direct liner *Parametta*. As two of the nine passengers aboard, they quickly became part of a friendly and congenial group, thoroughly enjoying the twenty-one-day voyage from San Francisco to Sydney.

It seemed that no matter to what far corner of the earth the Pococks journeyed, there were always old friends or new on hand to greet them. At Sydney it was Mrs. Merv Wood, wife of Australia's champion sculler, who was on the dock to welcome them to the land down under. She drove them to the Paramatta River, where her husband was competing in a regatta, then to the suburban Mansion Hotel at Kings Cross, where the Woods had reserved a room for them. Following a couple of days of sightseeing under the guidance of the Woods, the Pococks made the thirteen-hour trip by train from Sydney to Melbourne, where they were met by the Rev. Robert Burns, who informed them that they were to spend the night with him and his family. It seemed that a member of the Pococks' church in Seattle had visited the Burns family the previous year and had written them that George and Frances were coming for the Olympics. At Ballarat, where the Olympic rowing events were to be held on Lake Wendoree, George was quartered at the Olympic Village and Frances was delivered by the Rev. Burns to the home of Keith and Gladys Price. Keith was a member of the Ballarat Rowing Committee and, like the Burnses and the Pococks, belonged to the Christian Church. The arrangement proved a delightful one, and the two families remained close friends over the years.

At the Olympic Village, George also met his friend from the Canadian Commonwealth Games, William Stevenson. He was manager and coach of the New Zealand oarsmen, and, as George was to learn, the largest and wealthiest builder and general contractor in New Zealand. Stevenson insisted that the Pococks come to New Zealand after the Games.

Lake Wendoree was a small body of water, just long enough for a 2,000-meter course with four crews abreast. It was entirely covered by weeds, except for the race course, which was literally cut through the vegetation to accommodate the Olympic contenders. Again, the United States garnered its share of the Gold, placing first in three of the seven rowing events: the eights, pair with coxswain, and pair without cox.

Following a pleasant week with the Prices and another week touring Australia in a rented car, the Pococks responded to the barrage of telegrams from William Stevenson by booking a flight to Auckland. Since it wouldn't arrive until nearly midnight, George wired his friend not to bother meeting them at the airport, and giving him the name of the hotel where they would be staying. But the hospitable New Zealander greeted them at the airport, demanded their luggage from a porter who had been instructed to dispatch it to their hotel, and stowed it in the trunk of his large and shiny American automobile. "You're coming home with us," he announced in a voice that brooked no arguments.

They arrived at the Stevenson estate some miles outside Auckland in brilliant moon-light which gleamed on white paddock fences, and the sleek forms of a number of beautiful racehorses. When George voiced his admiration for them, Stevenson said, "You like 'em? I'll give you a couple." George observed later, "When I got to know Bill better, I realized that if I hadn't changed the subject in a hurry I would have ended up with a couple of New Zealand racehorses in our back yard in Seattle. Bill Stevenson was the most warm-hearted, generous man I have ever known."

The fortnight and more the Pococks spent with the Stevensons was one of the great experiences of their lives. Frances formed a warm friendship with Stevenson's wife Ruby, as she had with the Rev. Bobby Burns's wife in Australia. The two men became close chums, addressing each other after a day or two as George and "Alf." They spent glorious days trout fishing on Lake Rotoiti, where the Stevensons had a summer home and kept a motor launch, feasting on their catches grilled expertly by Alf, wrapped in wet newspapers and placed over driftwood embers on the beach. On one occasion, a launch approached their fishing spot crewed by three roughly dressed men, one of whom cupped his hands and shouted, "Have your licenses ready. We're coming to inspect." Alf, fishing from his launch, grinned at them and said, "Come aboard, mates, and have a spot," which they did with alacrity. Then he gave each of them a beautiful freshly-caught six-pound trout.

George, fishing from the shore, observed all this with some amazement. "I thought, this man Stevenson! His goodheartedness knows no bounds. Fancy treating three lake bums as generously as this." Then, he recalled, "After they had left, waving farewell, Alf sang out to me, 'Do you know who that was, George?' When I told him I didn't have the vaguest idea, he said, 'That was Mr. Holyoke, the Prime Minister of New Zealand.' 'Oh yes,' I replied, 'and I'm the Prince of Wales.' Fair dinkum, it was, but true. And one of the other rather scroungy looking men in the boat was Mr. Coles, who owned the posh lodge on the lake where England's Prime Minister (and old Eton oarsman), Anthony Eden, had come to regain his health."

They also visited several Stevenson construction jobs, including one at Kopoka where a hundred million yards of earth was being removed to uncover a fifty-foot-thick seam of coal, which was to be conveyed by endless bucket line to fuel a huge electrical generating plant. But most satisfying of all to George were his visits to St. George's Rowing Club a few miles from the Stevenson estate where Alf had a four, a pair, and two singles training for the New Zealand rowing championships.

He and Frances were delighted, while stopping over in Honolulu on the way home, to receive a cable from Stevenson: "Won four-oared and pair-oared championships."

"Good on him," George commented in true New Zealand style.

The Melbourne Olympics were the last that George and Frances attended. The XVII Olympiad of 1960 was held in Rome, and of it George recalled:

By now Stan was a very big factor in the shell building firm. He had graduated from the University of Washington a few years earlier with a degree in engineering, and despite tempting coaching offers, had decided to concentrate on shell building. I guess as a fourth generation member of a boatbuilding family, it was in his blood, and by 1960 he was taking over many of my responsibilities and instituting numerous improvements. We were again entrusted with the responsibility of building the seven shells for the U.S. Olympic crews, which we shipped from Seattle aboard an Italian freighter.

Stan accompanied the American crews to Rome. He had coached the Lake Washington Rowing Club fours and pairs with and without coxswain, all of which had qualified at the trials to represent the United States in Italy. Navy again represented America in the eight-oared event. Only one Gold Medal was taken that year; the four without cox, which Stan had coached.

United States crews did somewhat better in 1964 at Tokyo, with Gold medals won by the eight, manned by the Vesper Rowing Club of Philadelphia, and the pair with coxswain.

For the first time in many years, no Pocock-built shells were used by U.S. crews in the 1968 games at Mexico City. Cheaper foreign-built boats were substituted for the

George and Stan Pocock

lovingly crafted cedar masterpieces from the shores of Lake Washington. No gold medals were won by the United States that year, nor in the Munich Olympics four years later, where foreign shells were also used.

It was the beginning of a long decline in American world-class rowing, which had been dominant for more than three decades, and, sadly, in the production of the heart-liftingly beautiful, painstakingly hand-crafted wooden racing eights.

By 1970 America was abandoning the gold standard of stout ash and gleaming cedar for the age of plastics and mass production. After a half century as the acknowledged world leader in his chosen art, George decided it was time to retire.

10

Remembered Crews
and Coaches

I N 1972, at the age of eighty-one and semi-retired from the family boatbuilding
business which was being managed by his son Stan, George Pocock, at the insis-
tence of his family and friends, recorded many of his recollections of his sixty
years of rowing involvement. It was from these notes that much of the material for
this book was derived. His memories of crews and coaches are best told in his own
words.

The success of the crews under Rusty Callow continued, and there were many universities bidding for his services. In the fall of 1927 he finally succumbed to the offer of the
University of Pennsylvania. He would be very much missed at the University of Washington, whose crews he had led to national fame. He would be especially missed by me.
Rusty was a natural leader of men. He had the ability, it seemed, to look right into a
man. In all the time I knew him, he had never lost his temper or sworn at his men, but
they worked far harder for him than if he had. There was always great camaraderie
between Rusty and his oarsmen, a bond of love, for want of a better definition. I remember
in 1923, when we were making the four-day train trip to Poughkeepsie for our first
International Rowing Association regatta. One of the travel days was a Sunday, and
Rusty made arrangements with the conductor to use the dining car for church services.
The whole crew attended. Rusty delivered the sermon and Ray Morse, one of the varsity
oarsmen, read the lesson. This was no cursory affair, but was deep and genuine, and I
am sure the boys were uplifted by it.

While at Pennsylvania, Rusty became close friends with Buck Walsh, coach of the
Naval Academy crew. Buck was nearing the end of his career, and a few years later
when Rusty met with him for the last time, he was terminally ill. His dying request

George Pocock and Tom Bolles in coaching launch, Poughkeepsie (Life Magazine *photo*)

was that Rusty take over the Navy crew and carry on his work. Typically, Rusty complied with his old friend's last request, and continued to win honors for his crews and himself at Annapolis.

At Washington, the big question was who would be chosen to succeed the man who had made its varsity crews the most feared in the United States? There were many, many applicants, and actually I was consulted by Charles May, the faculty athletic chairman, who showed me the names of the applicants.[1] Among them was that of Alvin Ulbrickson, who had pulled stroke oar for Washington's freshman crew in 1923, and the varsity from 1924 through 1926. I told Mr. May that I thought Al Ulbrickson was the best choice. He was modest; he would listen and learn, and I believed, like Rusty Callow, had the makings of a good leader. The choice proved an excellent one, and he served well for thirty years.

1. George Pocock was an unpaid consultant in this area. H. W. McCurdy recalls that he got George's advice and counsel on each of five coaches he obtained over the years for MIT, and one for Columbia.

During that thirty years, a number of freshmen coaches worked with Ulbrickson. The first was Tom Bolles, the most successful freshman coach ever at Washington. He left in 1936 to become head coach at Harvard, where he had a most distinguished career. In his first season there, Harvard won all its races and wound things up by beating its traditional rival Yale, for the first time in years. After fifteen years as head coach, Tom was elevated to the position of athletic director, serving in that capacity for another twelve years, retiring in 1963. He then became the first person to be named director emeritus in recognition of his years of brilliant service to Harvard athletics. From freshman coach at Washington to athletic director emeritus at Harvard in twenty-seven years is proof of a working life well spent.

Bob Moch, one of Washington's outstanding coxswains, served as freshman coach before going to MIT as head coach, followed by Bud Raney, who left to become head coach at Columbia University. Then came Gus Erickson, who served for two years and left as head coach at Syracuse. The next appointee was our son Stan Pocock, who served six years as freshman coach, and whose crews rowed at Poughkeepsie five times, winning three of the races and placing second in the other two.

Fil Leanderson, who had succeeded Stan as freshman coach, took over as varsity coach upon the retirement of Al Ulbrickson. Leanderson served for seven years, and upon his retirement Stan was asked by Athletic Director Jim Owens to take over, but he had apparently inherited the family love for boatbuilding, and was deeply involved in the family business. He recommended Dick Erickson, who was hired. Dick has had three or four years at it now,[2] and rowing at Washington seems to be on the upgrade.

The coaches who were responsible for American Olympic Gold Medal successes I must list as I remember them:

Carroll M. Ebright has three Gold Medal Olympic victories to his credit: in 1928, 1932, and 1948. Ky was a hard worker on and off the water, devoting his heart and mind to his California crews almost every waking hour in season. His great concerns were always: Are the boats attaining the best speed in relation to the energy expended? Will the boys be rewarded with victory from what I have taught them, or are they knocking themselves out hopelessly? He studied every book written on rowing technique, using his own judgment as to what he would adopt or reject. I think his greatest crew was the one which took the gold at the 1932 Olympics in Long Beach, California. I was sitting next to some Italians in the grandstand who, of course, were rooting for their crew to win. As Ebright's crew sped by, one of them exclaimed, "Why it is a free-wheeling crew!" That described their stroke perfectly. The stroke man, Salisbury, took a terrific drive in one powerful cut; then eased slowly forward, letting the boat run free, and when it began to slow, whambo! Another one. Free-wheeling could not describe

2. Pocock wrote this in 1972. As of 1987, Dick Erickson is still in the job.

Dick Erickson

it better. So many crews will not let the boat run. They rush back and forth frantically, actually checking the run in the process.

Here I must take a little credit for Ky Ebright being a coach, because when Ben Wallis resigned as California crew coach in 1921, he wrote and asked me if I would tackle the job, and if not, would I recommend my choice from the list of applicants he had enclosed. I had to give the offer serious thought, for it was an attractive one, and to me a great honor as well. What finally tipped the scales was the knowledge that American rowing badly needed shells, and if I signed up with one university, rowing would suffer through lack of racing shells. Ky Ebright's name was on the list, and it was his I sent to Ben Wallis.

Dick Glendon of Navy was coach of the winning eight-oared shell in the 1920 Olympics. This was before my time on a national scale, and I know of him only by hearsay. He was a hard taskmaster, and a crew that gets only work and no laughs gets very touchy. He apparently realized this, and called in Jack Kelly, Sr., who was the United States single sculling entry, to cheer the midshipmen up. Jack was just the man to do it, for he was what young people nowadays call "laid back." The fear of being beaten

This group of University of Washington crew hopefuls, ca. 1914, contained three young oarsmen destined to become nationally known coaches. Lower arrow designates Ky Ebright; upper arrows, left to right, Rusty Callow and Ed Leader.

just wasn't in his makeup. His attitude of taking everything in stride, and with a laugh, was contagious. The Naval Academy crew caught it and went on to win the Gold. Two lines from Longfellow might be appropriate: *"They felt their hearts beat lighter/And leap onward with the stream."*

The 1931 University of Washington varsity crew. From left to right: Henry Schmidt, bow; Don Williamson; Herb Mjorud; Don Morris; Alton Phillips; Gil Bowen; Gordon Parrott; John Ginger, stroke; and Curly Harris, coxswain

In 1924 it was Ed Leader who coached Yale's Gold Medal winning crew in Paris. Ed was a former oarsman under Hiram Conibear and crew coach at Washington, and was also a tough taskmaster. His tactics, I think, were similar to those of an old-time sailing ship master who would whack a man over the head with a belaying pin if he did not obey instantly. He didn't go that far, of course, but verbally he could make a man feel less than the dust. He was a perfectionist, and his crews became perfection itself; a thing of beauty to watch, getting a beautiful run on the shell, which seemed to literally ghost along. Right here I must add that our present day crews seem to have lost the ability to get that run between strokes. They all look too hurried. The hallmark of a good crew, viewed from a distance, gave the impression that they had stopped rowing; then suddenly the oars would strike. Many say this may be all right for a three-mile race, but in fact champions at that distance were usually champions in 2,000-meter

Ky Ebright, 1933

Al Ulbrickson, 1933

events also. The classic stroke can be compressed into a faster clocking with the same percentage of drive and recovery.

The next coach on the Olympic Gold Medal list is Al Ulbrickson of Washington, whose crew won in Nazi Germany in 1936. That year the Husky crew had been aiming from the start for the honor of representing the United States at Berlin. Bob Moch was undoubtedly going to be coxswain. He had a rare instinct for skippering an eight-oared shell; more importantly, he had a tremendous spirit which spread the length of the boat. A winning spirit.

I built a new shell for the occasion, and we named it *Husky Clipper*. No one was designated to christen it, as I think it was paid for from university funds rather through

Unique crew race: in November 1941, two of Al Ulbrickson's University of Washington crews raced two Swinomish Indian war canoes at La Conner, Washington. The eight-oared Husky shells bested the Indian canoes with eleven paddlers.

a donation. Bob came up to the shop on the afternoon of the day it was to take to the water and said, "George, will you christen the shell?" I replied, "Sure, Bob. I will." Then I began to think: Berlin . . . Olympic Games . . . German . . . *sauerkraut!* I dashed up town and bought a can of sauerkraut juice. At the christening ceremony, with all the boys holding the shell ready for launching, I poured the juice over the bow with the words, "I christen this boat *Husky Clipper*. May it have success on all waters it speeds over. Especially in Berlin." The boys began to sniff, and one of them said, "It smells like sauerkraut." I replied, "It is . . . to get it used to Germany." They all laughed and nodded, and I am sure their spirits were lifted a little higher. That evening, what a workout! The *Husky Clipper* figuratively flew over the water.

I had remembered how the naming of an earlier shell had helped lift the minds and spirits of the Washington varsity crew of 1929, which was preparing to race the world champion California Bears, who had won the Olympic Gold the previous year at Amsterdam. For this event, I built a new shell, the first one ever planked with Alaska cedar, an ivory colored wood of great beauty. This one also had no official sponsor, or even a name. The day before the big race, the crew voted to name it *George Pocock*. Their decision warmed my heart, but instead of using that name, I figured it gave me a license to pick a name myself.

Since the distinctive wood with which it was sheathed came from Alaska, and in Seattle Alaska is associated with gold, I chose *Pay Streak*. That had also been the name given the amusement and concession area at the Alaska-Yukon-Pacific Exposition, held on the present university campus in 1909. Its carnival atmosphere and marvels such as the Igorote Village and the battle between the *Monitor* and the *Merrimac* had delighted the children, and many of the varsity oarsmen had heard of it from older brothers or sisters. *Pay Streak* was painted on the bow the night before race day, and I concealed the name until the boat was launched for the race. As the crew placed it on the water, I withdrew the covering and christened it *Pay Streak*. A few pleased grins and low whistles and they embarked, a gleam in their minds' eye. They rowed a splendid race against this world champion California crew, and won by about twelve feet.

Those Washington crews of the 1920s and 1930s provided an amazing number of outstanding coaches to universities all across America. Bob Moch, cox of the Olympic Gold Medal winning crew of 1936, was one, distinguishing himself as Washington freshman coach, and varsity coach at MIT. Another was Harrison Sanford, one of the young men who shared the flea-infested bed during Washington's first Poughkeepsie trip back in 1923. He coached Cornell's "Big Red" crew for many years, with his 1957 crew probably its greatest. Made up of all seniors, each oarsman was a master of his art, it won all its races that year; then on to Henley and an international triumph in the Challenge Cup race, the featured event of this legendary old regatta on the Thames. No college coach could have had a better season in a non-Olympic year.

Among the other Washington oarsmen who, after graduation, did their turns as coaches with great distinction were Bud Raney, Washington frosh and Columbia; Gus Erickson, Washington frosh and Syracuse; Loren Schoel, Marietta and Syracuse; Jim McMillin, MIT; Vic Michaelson, Syracuse frosh and Brown; Charles Logg, Rutgers; Gene Melder, Clark; Mike Murphy, Wisconsin; Dutch Schoch, Princeton; and Ellis MacDonald, Marietta.

Norman Sonju, another Washington graduate, was Harrison Sanford's freshman coach

Most of the oarsmen on this 1926 University of Washington National Championship crew became coaches at major universities across the nation. From left to right: Marius Glerup, bow; Jim Matthews (Pennsylvania); Norm Sonju (Wisconsin); Homer Kearns; Harold Condon; Jim Hart; Harrison Sanford (Cornell); Al Ulbrickson, stroke (Washington); Art Wuthenow, coxswain. Not pictured were Tom Bolles, bow (who later coached at Harvard), and Frank Blethen, coxswain, who were in the shell for the Princeton race that year.

at Cornell for many years, and was then appointed head coach at Wisconsin, where he enjoyed great success. His handicap there was the short rowing season. If there had been another month of rowing weather his crews would have won more IRA championships. Even so, Norm won a fair share of them. I always thought Norm could impart the ideal race-winning Washington stroke a little better than most.[3]

No listing of famous American rowing coaches would be complete without mention of Jim Ten Eyck, crew coach at Syracuse for thirty-five years, and certainly one of the most colorful of them all. Like a number of the early college coaches, he had been a professional sculler—one of the best in the country—and he was a hale and hearty eighty-six years of age when his Syracuse crews raced at Poughkeepsie in 1937. I remember that Jim had a passion for keeping his boats' performance secret prior to the race, taking his freshmen and varsity crews far down the river for their practice sessions, well away from any curious eyes.

We became good friends, and were walking down to the river one day from the Highland lodgings, when he suddenly put out his hand and stopped me. He said, "Follow me, George," and we left the path to follow a narrow trail until we came to a natural rock escarpment. He pulled aside some growing plants and there was a trickle of sparkling water coming out of the rock. There was a small can near by, which he filled and handed to me; a lovely cool drink of sweet water. He filled it again and drank, put the cup down and led the way back to the path. He said, "Do you know, George, that water has been flowing out of there for fifty years that I know of, because I took a drink there fifty years ago, and it's just as refreshing now as it was then." The memory of that small incident was a great help to me many years later.

In 1945, the city of Poughkeepsie held a banquet to celebrate the first half century of the national championship regattas there. Near noon of the day it was to be held, I was told that the coaches had selected me to be the speaker. I had been working long hours on the shells and my mind was totally occupied with the coming race. I tried to beg off, but with no luck. Seeking solitude behind a pile of timber at the old Dutton Lumber yard adjacent to the boathouse, I tried to think of what to say. Suddenly I recalled old Jim Ten Eyck's favorite water source of half a century. I told the story of our visit there, and added that from an equally mysterious source, young men have been pouring into Poughkeepsie for the last half century also, gathering health and strength rowing on the river; learning to pull their weight ever since, and consequently becoming fine citizens for the rest of their lives.

Jim Ten Eyck was a great story-teller as well as a great oarsman. On another of our visits together he told me of his race for a thousand dollar purse against a German sculler. The course was on the Hudson River, from the Battery on lower Manhattan to the New York Central railway bridge in Albany, a distance of 150 miles. Jim's father followed behind in a small motor boat. At Poughkeepsie, the halfway point, Jim was

3. The legendary (and undefinable) "Conibear Stroke" had been referred to later as the "Husky Stroke," and more generally, as the "Washington Stroke." As Washington oarsmen of the 1920s to 1940s took over the coaching of all but a half dozen major universities in the United States, it was referred to overseas as the "American Stroke." Even the venerable *Encyclopaedia Britannica* accepted the myth that Hiram Conibear "developed at the University of Washington, aided by the Pocock brothers, expert builders and riggers of racing shells, a system that by the 1940s dominated college rowing east and west."

well ahead and feeling bushed. He rolled out onto a dock for a brief rest. His father came alongside and gave him a drink of brandy, which made him sick as well as tired. But the oars of his rival were flashing in the near distance and, sick as he was, Jim got back aboard and sculled over to the highland side. As he crept along the shore, with the German coming up fast astern, he saw a trickle of that blessed riverside water trickling out of the rocks on the other side of the railroad tracks. He hailed a track-walker, who brought him a can of it, and Jim took a long swig. After thanking the railroad worker, he continued on, joyfully feeling his health and strength building with every stroke. Completely restored, he finished the race about an hour ahead of his opponent, his total elapsed time for the 150-mile pull against the river current, approximately twenty-two hours.

I asked him if he had any ill effects from this long effort, and he said he had to stay in Albany two days as he couldn't straighten up; walked as though he had a piano on his back. About a week after he got home, all the skin on the inside of his hands sloughed off like gloves, and he nailed them to the boathouse door. The race and its aftermath received a lot of publicity, and the then President of the United States, Teddy Roosevelt, wired him an invitation to come to the White House and tell him about it personally, which Jim did, spending considerable time with the sports-loving President. The shell Jim used now hangs in the National Museum in Washington.

A favorite Ten Eyck story involved a big, muscular freshman who turned out for crew at Syracuse, where Jim was coaching. The recruit was put on a rowing machine, but the friction belt was loose and there was little or no resistance on the handle. The freshman tightened the screw. He apparently didn't know his own strength, for when he tried again it was so tight that he could hardly move the handle. He gave a vicious lunge, the handle broke, and he fell over backward, striking his head on the floor so forcefully that he knocked himself unconscious. At this point, Jim arrived on the scene and was told that the muscular youth had pulled so hard he broke the stout oar handle. Obviously impressed, Jim said, "Bring him to quickly and put him in a boat."

A colorful contemporary of Ten Eyck was Fred A. Plaisted, who died in 1946 at the age of ninety-six as the world's oldest sculling champion, having won the world professional championship in 1877 against Ten Eyck and a great black oarsman, "Frenchy" Johnson. Plaisted later coached crew at Yale, Harvard, Columbia, and Bowdoin. At the age of eighty-nine, he raced Olympic medal winner Jack Kelly over a mile and a quarter course on the Schuylkill River. Kelly won, but Plaisted gave him a run for his money. He was active as boatman for Philadelphia rowing clubs until just before his death. When confronted with the old myth that oarsmen die young, George would gently mention Ten Eyck and Plaisted, adding a bit of color to the medical statistics which show ex-crewmen have longer average life spans than non-oarsmen. George also had fond memories of Naval Academy Coach Buck Walsh:

Jack Kelly and family on the occasion of Jack Jr.'s win in the Diamond Sculls at Henley, 1947. The future Princess Grace of Monaco is on the left.

In 1947, Buck Walsh was the Naval Academy coach. He was, in common with all coaches on the eve of a major race, worried about his crew. He invited me out in his launch to watch them at work and I told him they looked good to me. After the practice runs, Buck enlisted a couple of other oarsmen and we went out in a four-oared shell with me at stroke and Buck at Number 3. He was pulling like mad, and I advised him to ease up a bit, and be sure to catch right on the dot. He did, and the boat immediately started to swing beautifully. Buck was as pleased as a kid with a new toy. He said, "That's the first time I have seen a boat go faster through a man easing up a bit." He had been guilty of the sin of being a "stopper." I have seen many "stoppers" in eight-oared crews, and the results have always been bad.

Buck Walsh and I spent most of that afternoon together, and toward evening we strolled up town and went in to have an ice cream soda, talking rowing all the time. In the ice cream parlor, oblivious of the other customers, who probably thought we had been out in the sun too long, we sat on the floor, demonstrating to each other the movements we thought right for the most effective stroke: smooth flowing actions and keep the noise and fuss down. Incidentally, Buck's Navy crew won the race that year.

Buck was also something of a practical joker. He and Rusty Callow were great friends, and Buck told Rusty one summer that he had a super athlete coming to the Academy that fall, who had already signed up for crew. From the sheer riot of his imagination, Buck described him as a younger brother of heavyweight boxing champion Jack Dempsey; well over six feet tall, weighing 190 pounds, and able to do fifty pushups with one arm. Rusty was deeply impressed, and doubtless somewhat worried. That fall he scanned the sports pages to read about Buck's good fortune, but found not a word about the potential super-star. In the spring, when college rowing began again and Rusty and Buck met, Rusty immediately wanted to know about Jack Dempsey's kid brother who was supposed to be pulling an oar for Navy. Buck, who had forgotten all about his tall tale of the previous year, looked blank and asked "Who?" Rusty said, "Jack Dempsey's brother, of course. You told me about him last year." "Oh," said Buck, making a fast recovery. "He's coming next year."

Buck's Navy crew won at Poughkeepsie that year, and when Rusty heartily congratulated him Buck came back with a classic reply that seemed to sum up the frequent frustrations of coaches in that highly competitive sport . . . "It was great, but you know, I still don't think the joy of winning makes up for all the griefs I've had in losing."

Those great coaches of rowing's glory days were certainly diverse and highly individualistic men, but they had certain qualities in common. Technical knowledge of rowing is only part of the stock in trade of a good coach, and probably not the most important one at that. Hiram Conibear, who could hardly row at all when he took over as crew coach at Washington, is a case in point. He had to learn as he taught, but he launched Washington crews on their course to national and world fame. .

Rowing is perhaps the toughest of sports. Once the race starts, there are no time-outs, no substitutions. It calls upon the limits of human endurance. The coach must therefor impart the secrets of the special kind of endurance that comes from the heart and the mind and the muscles. I think my dad's admonition summed it up well. When Dick and I were youngsters racing singles on the Thames he always told us, "Think positively all the way to the finish line; never let a negative thought enter your mind . . . especially if you are behind."

Every good rowing coach, in his own way, imparts to his men the kind of self-discipline required to achieve the ultimate from mind, heart, and body. Which is why most ex-oarsmen will tell you they learned more fundamentally important lessons in the racing shell than in the classroom.

But for all the color and dedication of the great rowing coaches, the *New York Herald-Tribune* sports writer covering the 1936 Poughkeepsie Regatta was moved to write: "The most interesting character on the Hudson isn't the octogenarian, Ten Eyck; the sturdy son of old England Jim Wray, nor the venerable Dick Glendon. He is Seattle's George Pocock."

11

The Later Years

I N 1963, when George was seventy-two, he left the University of Washington
campus where, in the course of more than half a century, he had become an
almost legendary figure. The firm of George Pocock Racing Shells, Inc., which
had moved from the original World War I seaplane hangar to quarters in the Conibear
Shellhouse which replaced it, moved again to a larger boatshop on neighboring Lake
Union.

Of the master boatbuilder in these later years, *The Northwest* magazine provided
this description: "He bears a striking physical resemblance to the poet, Carl Sandburg;
the same craggy features, a not-quite unruly shock of white hair, the indifferent gait
of a man utterly confident in his command of a medium. And, yes, one might say
that both men, in their different ways, are brothers poet laureate."

He remained trim and stood ramrod straight; his favorite exercise still was sculling
vigorously on the waters of Lake Washington.

Over his half-century of shell building in Seattle, there had been gradual changes
in the materials and design of the finished product, but none in the standards of
workmanship or the mellow atmosphere of the shop, which remained the antithesis
of the noisy, hurry-up, assembly line stereotype of the American manufacturing plant.
His crew of hand-picked craftsmen, headed by octogenerian Hilmar Lee, moved with
deliberation around the skeletons of slim boats, walking slowly and handling tools
carefully in an atmosphere of profound tranquility. And the master craftsman himself
never moved through his shop without pausing somewhere along the way to sand

145

Workers in the shellhouse, 1953

down a barely visible rough spot on some half-finished shell, or to tighten a screw not quite set to his standards.

Probably the most significant change in the basic construction between the Pocock shells of 1963 and those of 1913 was the elimination of dozens of ribs to which the

Dr. Alfred Strauss, who had met and hosted Washington's first national champion crew in Chicago in 1923, is hosted by George Pocock nearly a half century later in Seattle at christening ceremonies of a new Husky shell named for Strauss.

cedar "skin" of earlier boats had been attached. In an eight-oared shell approximately sixty feet long, there had been sixty ribs sawn from 3/8-inch birch plywood. Their elimination reduced shell weight by some eight pounds, but that wasn't a major factor. The real advantage was in the fact that the ribless shells presented an absolutely clean, even line to the water.

"Ribs have been our nemesis for years," George explained, "because they frequently cause unevenness of the outer skin." While he refused to go into technical details of what was certainly a major trade secret, he explained that the ribless boats were made possible by what he called a "cedar sandwich," with fiber glass applied over both the inside and outside of the boat's skin, so thinly as to be absolutely transparent. It required a well trained eye to distinguish between the old style of shells and the new.

Three generations of boatbuilders. Top row, left to right: son Stan; George; Rick Van Winkle; grandson Chris; Jerry Norman; Bob Brunswick; cousin Don Norman; Harry Kirschner; brother-in-law Ed Van Mason. Bottom row: Dan Raetzloff, Mike Rados, Gary Rathe, Norman Koskela, Denny Deusen

The workmanship and materials which produced Pocock racing shells at the time of the shop's location change were described in *The Northwest:*

A racing shell that comes out of the Pocock factory is the very model of functional design and construction. Its hull possesses not a single degree of excess curvature, not an ounce of useless weight. Each of the many species of wood that are wedded to form the whole is chosen not only for its aesthetic value, but for a special physical quality. Yet the natural colors peculiar to the woods make the finished craft a thing of remarkable beauty.

The keel is made of sugar pine from California and Oregon, because sugar pine will not rot and has a capacity for holding nails well. The hull is formed from cinnamon-colored western red cedar, each side having been shaved from the same piece to 11/64 of an inch. Because they are cut from the same plank, the sides swell or contract equally, thus reducing the possibility of warping. Matched Alaska cedar, as golden as honey, goes into the wash boards (gunwale) to keep the boat straight. Rigger timbers are tough eastern ash out of New York and Pennsylvania, as are the stretchers, those shoe-clad footboards that can be adjusted to different leg lengths for individual rowers. Seats that are shaped to fit the rump bones are a laminate of red cedar and sugar pine. Rudders are cut from multi-hued mahogany plywood. Sweeps—that is, the oars—call for two special woods also: Englemann spruce from Montana and Australian ironbark, "the closest thing to metal that grows." (Not really bark, as the name implies.)

Oar shafts and blades are spruce—a wood strong in tension, weak in compression—backed up at the join by a strip of almost black ironbark, which imparts spring and compressive strength to the oar. True spring metal has been tried, George explains, but proved to be too stiff for the job. Ironbark, a log of which will sink in water, is used ordinarily for tugboat sheathing and in archery bows.

"However, it is very vital to sweeps," George says, "because it gets them out of the water fast."

The nearly transparent top surface of the enclosed ends of a shell is fiber glass cloth impregnated with varnish or polyurethane. Too, the exterior of the thin red cedar hull is reinforced with a finer woven glass cloth—silk stocking sheer, says George's son Stan—while the interior of the shell is covered with cloth of a heavier weave. (Forming George Pocock's rib-eliminating "cedar sandwich.)

The finished product—the racing eight—was not breathtakingly fast in comparison to motorized racing vehicles, but on a per-horse-power basis, George insisted, its performance was impressive. "A shell averages about twelve miles an hour," he explained. "A man is rated at one-tenth maximum horsepower. Twelve miles an hour over the water with 4/5 of one horsepower is pretty fast."

As early as 1948, when George made his second trip to the Olympic Games as chief boatman for the American crews, he had been given the prestigious award of Seattle Man of the Year in Sports. In later years, as his influence spread throughout the international rowing fraternity and he became more and more in demand as an inspirational speaker at major gatherings, more honors came his way.

In 1952 the big main room at the newly constructed Northeast Seattle YMCA in his beloved University District was dedicated as the George Pocock Room. The ceremonies included the unveiling of an oil painting of George by Walter Isaacs, head of the University of Washington art department. Fred Laudan, vice president of Boeing, spoke of George as an internationally famed builder; Al Ulbrickson of his qualities as a builder of sportsmanship; and the Rev. John Paul Pack, his minister at University Christian Church, on his contributions as a builder of character. "Congratulations to

Stan Pocock at work on a shell (photo by T. M. Green)

the Builder'' were extended by Washington Governor Arthur B. Langlie and H. P. Everest, acting president of the University of Washington.

George responded with his usual modesty. "If I deserve a room," he said, "there are men here who deserve a whole building. I'm only a part of everyone I ever met."

And he concluded with a touch of the reverence which was also an integral part of his character: "If I could choose a line to put under that portrait. I'd quote the verse, 'These hands, O Lord, I dedicate to thee.'"

Four years later, the University Christian Church honored him at its annual meeting with a "This Is Your Life" surprise ceremony patterned after the popular television show of that time. The outline of his life, from childhood on the Thames, was printed in a beautifully bound book, which was presented to him by the Rev. Pack, who also read a series of testimonials from sports and church leaders including Royal Brougham, *Post-Intelligencer* sports editor; Bob Moch, University of Washington Olympic crew coxswain, representing generations of Husky oarsmen; Al Ulbrickson, representing the nation's crew coaches; and Ray Farwell, Jr., manager of Swedish Hospital, representing former members of George's longtime Sunday school class.

Also in 1956, George was the recipient of the second annual Rowing Citation Award for outstanding contributions to the sport of rowing at Poughkeepsie. His citation called him "probably the best loved man in the sport of rowing."

In the summer of 1963 the University of Washington Board of Rowing Stewards held its Appreciation Night, honoring George as a "true friend, wise counselor, and world renowned designer and builder of racing shells." The accompanying record of his life and achievements concluded, "Let us close with his own words—which, in a shell or building it, George Pocock exemplifies—'If it's worth doing—it's worth doing well.'"

In January 1969, a couple of months before his seventy-eighth birthday, George was a guest of honor at the National Rowing Foundation's annual Awards Dinner at the Biltmore Hotel in New York, where he was inducted into the Helms Rowing Hall of Fame. This is the highest accolade which can be bestowed by the United States rowing fraternity, and George's pleasure was made greater by the fact that the other Hall of Fame inductee that year was his long-time friend, H. W. McCurdy. There was a touch of sadness, too, for the thoughts of both turned to Mac's son Tom, who had sat at the master's feet in the Conibear Crewhouse to absorb the lore of rowing, and had died as a result of Korean war naval service. It was the Pocock-built eight-oared shell *Spirit of Tom McCurdy* which was to be rowed by Dick Erickson's Husky crew in the upcoming Pan American Games at Cali, Colombia.

Following the ceremonies, McCurdy urged George to begin writing down the highlights of his life and career as the now-acknowledged patriarch and prophet of amateur rowing in America and much of the world. It was typical of George that he should protest that his achievements had been far too modest to warrant a published biography. "But if it should ever be done," he told McCurdy with his gentle smile, "I know what I should like the title to be. To me the most heart-stirring words of all are the

The dedication of the Tom McCurdy. *From left to right: Coach Dick Erickson, H. W. McCurdy, George Pocock, Athletic Director Joe Kearny*

ones the coxswain barks as the oarsmen flex their muscles and the starter raises his arm, and in every shell eight hearts beat as one . . . 'READY ALL!' "

Writing in *Sports Illustrated* in the early 1960s, William Worden marveled that "for all the intricacies of construction, the improvements, the painstaking labor and the servicing of boats once they are in use, the price for an eight-oared shell is still only $1,800, or exactly $550 more than what the same craft sold for in the depths of the Depression. Pocock is typically reticent about his yearly gross. 'It's too mundane from my point of view. I could charge double for these shells and get it. I'm sure anyone would be astonished at how low my gross actually is.'

George Pocock presents award to the prize-winning four, Lakeside School, Seattle, ca. 1970. From left to right: Rolfe Watson, Franklin "Pat" Smith, Pocock, John Rose, Scott McIntyre

"To George Pocock," Worden continued, "the moderate income rowing has given him is more than offset by the lifetime of interest he has had from it. It is enough for him that he was able, comfortably, to raise a son and daughter in a rather old-fashioned house in Seattle's Laurelhurst district, from which he always can look down on Lake Washington and frequently may see there the patterns made by boats he has created."

The simple fact was that George believed in the benefits of rowing to mind and body as simply and sincerely as he believed in God. Few men were less driven by greed and personal ambition, and by the 1960s he had found a new rationalization for cutting his profits, as the *Sports Illustrated* article explained:

"One reason he has kept his price low, Pocock says, is the rising interest in high school rowing. There are, he guesses, 60 high schools in the country conducting rowing programs, and he believes the number is growing all the time. 'The future of

American rowing is in the high schools,' he says, and on this subject he is positively loquacious. 'Oh, brother, what a chance there is. How those boys take to it. More than 160 boys showed up for a rowing turnout at Lincoln, Roosevelt and Lakeside here in Seattle. Last year we received orders from three other high schools in Poughkeepsie. They wanted eight-oared shells. Rowing is the best kind of high school activity.' "

In his conclusion, Worden tried to sum up the deep spiritual affinity George had for rowing:

"Pocock also has something of a mystical feeling about the sport, and in the end it is probably this which is responsible for his devotion. When he tries to explain his feeling he goes about the task obliquely. He says, 'What does rowing have? That's hard to answer; but I had a letter a year or so ago from a crewman who had gone on from Seattle to the Air Force. When he wrote to me, he'd just flown a jet. He told me that the only thing he could say about jet flying was that it's almost exactly like the feeling you get when an eight-oared shell is really swinging. I'm still not being specific. But in a sport like this—hard work, not much glory, but still popular in every century—well there must be some beauty which ordinary men can't see, but extraordinary men do.'

"George Pocock can see that beauty."

By 1970, George had turned over most of the responsibility for day-to-day operation of the family boatbuilding corporation to Stan, while keeping a loving but not always approving eye on latter-day developments in the oldest and most traditional of all intercollegiate sports. It was the age of Vietnam and Watergate, of protest and violence. The ancient verities were falling everywhere, and it was a sad thing to the man who had become the poet and prophet of rowing to see the changes in the sport and the craft to which he had devoted his life. His philosophies and techniques, accepted over the decades by crews and coaches to become the very fabric of oared racing, were being rejected by a new generation enamored of "beef and technology."

The beef was represented in the increasing size and weight of varsity crews, with many of the oarsmen from six feet five to six feet seven in height and well over two hundred pounds in weight. George believed that the massive muscles and sheer weight of a defensive linebacker or professional wrestler were more than likely to be a handicap rather than an advantage in a racing shell: "Rowing a race is an art, not a frantic scramble. It must be rowed with head power as well as muscular power." Too much beef, too much muscle was, he was convinced, likely to break the very essence of

The sixty-one foot shell occupies a lot of cabin space in the Boeing jetliner on its journey to Kansas City, 1969.

successful racing—the long, smooth "run" of the shell. The ideal candidate for a seat on a varsity crew, he believed, should be about six feet tall with a weight of less than two hundred pounds, and smooth-limbed, not bulging with muscle.

The technology, even more disturbing to the traditionalist, was the growing popularity of "synthetic" shells and oars made from carbon fibres. George was, as he had always been, a firm believer in the mystic blending of wood, water, and human heart and spirit which was the art of rowing.

Many years earlier, soon after the University of Washington crew under Al Ulbrickson had won the Berlin Olympic race for the United States, George had written an essay on rowing and the art of shell building for the U.S. Naval Academy *Log*. Even then, racing shells of non-wood construction were on the market. George gave them short shrift:

> A racing eight-oared shell is one article that will not yield successfully to the march of metal. Metal shells have repeatedly been tried in the United States, England and Germany; probably many other countries too, but the writer knows of the aforementioned efforts and is familiar with the results. Aluminum or duraluminum constructed shells have proven too lifeless, absolutely dead, and a good shell has to have life and resiliency to get in harmony with the swing of the crew.
>
> Therein lies the secret of successful crews: their "swing," that fourth dimension of rowing, which can only be appreciated by an oarsman who has rowed in a swinging crew, where the run is uncanny and the work of propelling the shell a delight. We believe that the nature of wood used in the construction has no little to do with this all-important phase.

By the mid-1970s, though, several firms were producing racing shells of fiberglass: and selling them in increasing numbers. They weighed about the same as the traditional wooden ones, 250 to 300 pounds for a 61-by-2-foot eight, but with the increasing scarcity and cost of the premium woods used in Pocock shells, the "plastic" models began to enjoy a price advantage. Ease of maintenance was another major selling point. In rowing as in yachting, boat owners turned from the warmth and beauty of wood to the assembly-line blandness of fiberglass. The wooden boat requires tender, loving care, including much scraping, sanding, polishing, and varnishing. Like the family car, the family boat made of fiberglass requires only an occasional washdown.

A few years later, an inventive Californian brought forth a shell made of Kevlar, a DuPont carbon fiber material developed originally to strengthen truck tires. Costing in the neighborhood of nine thousand dollars in 1979, these products of "space-age technology" weigh only 185 pounds. The theory was that if eight oarsmen have that much less weight to propel, they can cover a two-thousand-meter course faster and with less effort than their competitors.

Pocock shells being shipped to the East

George was wise enough to know that the sweet science of rowing an eight-oared racing shell resists such simple formulae. No one had proven that a lighter shell guaranteed faster times, and he felt that it didn't, or at best that it was only one factor in the complex physics of weight, displacement, and properly applied power at the oar blades. In his 1937 article in the Navy *Log,* he expressed his opinion in this regard: "Extreme cases of lighter boats have been built with very doubtful advantage; speed depends on a ship keeping its lines within certain limits, and a shell must be heavy enough to do this. If it is not, there is no advantage in lesser weight. Vanderbilt's America's Cup winner this year was many tons heavier than her adversary, and carried less sail area, but she was a faster boat."

But by the end of the 1970s, carbon fiber shells, often propelled by dull gray carbon fiber oars, were dominating rowing regattas across the country. Commenting on the technological changes prior to the 1979 regatta of the Eastern Association of Rowing Colleges, William N. Wallace wrote in the *New York Times:* "The esthetics

Christening the eight-oared shell George Pocock, *presented to the University of Washington by the Pocock family, 1976*

of this garbage is terrible. What more handsome place could an oarsman ever find than a boat house filled with the magnificence of the Pocock products from the bright of the varnished northwest woods in shells and oars which did not change for five decades, so perfect were they for this sport. And they may be still."

George did not live to see the final flowering of the plastic age in his beloved sport, but he would surely have agreed with Wallace's conclusion that "it seems to this person that technology's inroads into rowing remain small, thankfully. Regardless of carbon fibers, Kevlar or weight reduction, the athletes still count the most." Or, as George had put it long ago, "There are no fast boats: only fast crews."

And when Yale beat Penn by three lengths to win the Blackwell Cup that same year, the Eli's bow man, Ted Jaroszewiz, said: "It's not the boat. It's the people who row the boat."

George was gone then, but the rowing gospel he had preached for sixty years remained in the hearts and minds of a new generation of oarsmen.

And that was his ultimate victory.

George Yeoman Pocock died at Seattle on March 19, 1976, four days short of his eighty-fifth birthday. At the end, his words were of trust in God and gratitude for the loving family and dear friends who had abundantly blessed his life. The closing words of the memorial services at the University Christian Church were, fittingly, his rowing creed, given spontaneously some years earlier when he was asked to say a few words at the conclusion of a film on rowing:

It's a great art, is rowing.
It's the finest art there is.
It's a symphony of motion.
And when you're rowing well
Why it's nearing perfection—
And when you reach perfection
You're touching the Divine.
It touches the you of you's
Which is your soul.

Appendix A

THIS SUMMARY of George Pocock's theories regarding rowing technique was given to H. W. McCurdy by Jim Matthews in 1977. It was compiled for Rusty Callow during his tenure as crew coach at Pennsylvania in response to an inquiry about the most efficient leg drive, and is probably the best summary available of Pocock's opinions on the mechanics of successful crew racing.

Some Notes on Rowing by George Pocock

We have found the cardinal sin in rowing is throwing the shoulders at the beginning of the stroke while holding the slide still. You simply cannot develop rhythm or even keep the boat steady, as it is merely a body movement, one cannot get any pull on the oar. It is like being in a tug of war with the team standing full upright, you cannot pull. Here is the latest proven action—When the reach for the catch is got (not too much, just comfortable without stretching too much), feel for the water as it were, not coached to "miss no water" as it is impossible to miss no water. Better, miss as little as possible so as not to stop the way of the boat. If a crew is coached to miss no water they have to drop them in and stop the way of the boat, as you cannot bring the blade vertically down and pull at the same time. That is an impossibility and is stultifying to any thinking boy. Better not to coach at that point at all, I believe, unless they get to missing too much water.

When this reach for the catch is obtained the body angle must not change, but the slide must move and the legs go onto it with the body kept at the same angle as at the catch. As the oar reaches the right angle position to the boat, the back starts up and the elbows break so as to keep that blade going through in one cut. If the arms are kept straight at the point when the oar is at right angle to the boat, the oarsman has to coast over this dead point and then a long finish to get any work in. The object is to get as much effectual stroke in in the shortest time so that there is time for the gravy, the slow recovery, and the long run of the boat. It keeps a crew from getting a hard finish; a hard finish will probably make a boat go a little faster but at too much expense to the stamina of the man.

The boat is going fastest at the finish of the stroke, and that is where it should be nursed, to punch it from there is fatal. We found in building speed boats at Boeing that to increase speed from 30 to 35 miles an hour it took almost half as much power again, so it takes too much power to try and increase the speed of your eight at the finish of the stroke.

It is well to bear in mind, and to teach the boys, that the oar blade in effect suscribes an arc of a circle, in reality the blade moves very little but the effect is the same. The dangerous point in that arc is the high point or dead center. That is the point where the blade must be kept moving, otherwise you are going to get a double stroke. Before the high point and after the high point you must go through that high point by breaking the elbows down and getting one cut at it and therefore a shorter time in the water and loads of time for recovery.

I saw Washington's 1938 crew rowing 32 at Wisconsin, and it looked as though they were rowing 28, they had so much time. This is the natural way to row, Russell, and if a lad is not coached too much he will more or less drop into this style. Of course he has to be told originally, but it is no trouble to keep this style. Most coaches coach too much. There have been as many races lost through overcoaching as undercoaching. When there is too much megaphone a man thinks it is all style and no pulling that get a boat along.

This "one cut stroke" is not a loafing stroke but takes a lot of pulling, and if every one is doing his bit it's easy on everybody.

I always think that if a coach pounds on the ratio of one in the water and two out of the water, most everything else falls in line. So, Russell, you will see by foregoing description you are right in starting your slide with the leg drive, it has to be, but don't throw your shoulders in doing it. Keep them at the still forward position until the blade is under full pressure, then bring them over.

This is only answering the question of leg drive and I hope I have made myself clear. When that slide starts moving it keeps going all the way back until the legs are flat, but those legs must go down slowly. Don't whang them down, otherwise the leverage is not being carried out to the blade, as the tail must not shoot back.

Appendix B

THE FOLLOWING is a complete list of all University of Washington varsity lettermen in crew from 1903 through 1983. (* indicates team captain)

Some of the younger athletes listed below never knew George, but they were influenced by him nevertheless. As Rick Clothier, rowing coach at Annapolis, points out, "George's legacy was his disciples! By this I mean the countless coaches who learned their 'craft' literally at George's knee . . . 70 to 85 percent of all U.S. coaches were former University of Washington oarsmen. These men took the 'Pocock Style' out to nearly every American rowing college and university; thus not only did the Pocock boat rule the rowing world, so did the Pocock Style."

Many of those Pocock "disciples" turned coach are among those Washington varsity oarsmen of eight decades listed here. And as Coach Clothier also points out, an oarsman may be a generation removed—and still be a disciple of George Pocock.

Fred McElmow	03,04	Hart Willis	07,08	Bill Godfrey	09,10
Clint Lantz	03,04	Bart Lovejoy	07,08,09*	George Mohr	09
Dan Pullen	03,04,05	George Sadler	07	Lyman Shotwell	10
Carl Van Kurhan	03,04	Walt Dunbar	07,11,14	Paul Buwaldo	10
Orin Crim	03,04	Arthur O'Neal	08,09	Walter Wand	10,11
Guy Tilten	05	Arthur Aarr	08	Royal Pullen	10,11,12*
Dick Gloster	05,07*	Brous Beck	08,09,10	Henry Tiedje	10,11*
F. L. O'Brien	07,08,09*	Ev Thomsen	08,09	John Sommersett	11
Homer Kirby	07,08*	Doak Lowry	08	Levi Carrol	11
Paul Jarvis	07	Hal Wyckoff	09,10	Newton Smith	11
		Claude Catlin	09,11,14		

Hal Waller	11,12,13,15	Talbot Campbell	19	Bill Wohlmacher	27,28
Newell Wright	12	Otis Richardson	19	Marius Glerup	26,27,28*
Joe Morgan	12	Dave Kronfield	19,20	Myron Scott	27
Larry Wright	12	Leroy Berque	19,20	Ron Wailes	27,28
Will Ruggers	12	Chuck Logg	19,20,21*	Ellis MacDonald	27,28,29*
Clark Will	12,15	Char. Magnuson	20,21	Paul Orr	28,29
Ed Taylor	12,13*	Louis Nederlee	20,21	Bert Kauffman	27
Art Campbell	12	Swan Nord	20	Bob Schoettler	28
Paul Hammer	13,15	Newman Clark	20	Jack Valentine	28
Jim Frankland	13,14	Rowland France	21,24	Stan Valentine	28,29
Ed Leader	13,16	Robert Ingram	21,22	George Oistad	28
Archie Campbell	13	Sam Shaw	21,22,23*	Jim Beckstead	28
Elmer Leader	13	George Murphy	21,22*	Warren Davis	28,29,30*
Parker Bonney	13	Don Grant	22,23,24*	Ed Anderson	29
George Hutton	13	Pat Tiomarsh	22,23	Wally Litchfield	29,30
Larry Sexton	13	Virgil Murphy	22	John Ginger	29,30,31
Max Walske	13,14,16	Al Skibeness	22	Dick Odell	29,30
Geo. Schwabland	13	Wright Parkins	22,23	Gilbert Bowen	29,30,31
Clint Lee	13	Ed Cushman	22	Acton Phillips	29,30,31
A. C. Campbell	13	Lloyd Mason	22	Don Morris	29,30,31
Hank Zimmer-man	13,14,15*	Fred Spuhn	22,23,24	Henry Schmidt	29,31
Clyde Brokaw	14,15,16*	Max Luft	23,24,25*	Gerald Accorn	29,30
Clyde Rose	14	Charles Dunn	23	Karl Reese	30
Tom Cushman	14,15	Dow Walling	23,24,25	Loren Schoel	30,32
Hal Schumacher	14	H. J. Dutton	23,24,25	Richard Harris	29,30,31*
Russell Callow	14,15*	Harrison Sanford	24,25,26	Don Williamson	31,32
Art Ward	15	Homer Kerns	24,26	Herb Mjorud	31,32,33*
Paul McConihe	15,16,17	Hal Condon	24,25,26	Gordon Parrott	31,32,33*
Adolph Harr	15,16	Al Ulbrickson	24,25,26*	Charles Noble	31,32
Ward Kumm	14,16,17*	Art Wuthenow	25,26	Arthur Gobler	32
Chuck Newton	16,17	Jim Matthews	25,26	Herb Day	32,33
Ky Ebright	16,17	Norm Sonju	25,26,27*	Clarence Edmunson	32
Karey Whitney	17	Walt Malone	25	Pete Lewis	32
T. Brandenthaler	17,19,20	Tom Quast	25,27	Ed Ulbrickson	32
Brall Briggs	16,17	Jim Hart	25,26,27	Joe McCarthey	32
Wilbert Slemmons	17	Herb Morcom	25	Gregg Wilson	32
Almon Bogards	17,20	Frank Blethen	26,27	Ed Argersinger	32,33,34*
Russ Nagler	19,20,21	Charles McGuiness	27	Harvey Love	33,34
Walt Northfield	19	Tom Bolles	26	Walter Raney	33,34,35
Herman Luft	19,21	Frank Shaw	27	Robert Snider	33,34,35
		Joel Olmstead	27,28	Wilbur Washburn	33,34

Name	Years	Name	Years	Name	Years
Bob White	33,34,35*	Ellis Coder	39	Bob McFarlane	46
Ed Moore	34	Dallas Duppenthaler	39,40	Ed Gibson	46
Victor Carter	34	Gerald Keely	39,40	Chuck Brown	47,48
Frank Marolich	34	Charles Jackson	39,40,41*	Bill Harrah	47
Bud Schacht	35,36	Wayne Gordon	39,40	Bob Martin	47,48
Roger Morris	35,36,37	Bob Grunboch	39	Don Landon	47,48,49
Bob Green	35	Paul Soules	39,40*	Berny Benthin	47
Delos Schoch	35,36,37	Don Canfield	39	Stan Pocock	47
Charles Hartman	35,36,37	Bob Johnson	39	Bob Lee	47,48
Joe Rantz	35,36,37	Fred Colbert	39,40	Ed Hearing	48,49
George Hunt	35,36,37	Ted Garhart	40,41,42	John Audett	48,49,50
George Lund	35,36,37	Dick Yantis	40	Bob Young	47,48,49,50
George Morry	35	Al Erickson	40	Norm Buvick	47,48,49,50*
Charles Day	35,36,37	John Bracken	40,41,42*	Rod Johnson	47,48,49,50*
Walter Bates	35,36*	Vic Fomo	40,41,42	Manford McNeill	47
James McMillin	35,36,37*	Barton Douglas	40	Bob Harris	47
Sydney Lund	35,36	Bob Vincent	40	Dave Dixon	47
John York	35,37	Orwin Thomas	40	C. McCarthy	48,49,50
Bob Moch	35,36	Paul Simdars	40,41	Warren Westlund	
Donald Hume	36,37,38	Bill Neill	40,41		47,48,49,50*
John White	36,37,38	Doyle Fowler	41,42	Bob Will	48,49
Gordon Adam	36,37,38*	Walt Wallace	41,42	Gordon Giovanelli	48,49
Merton Hatch	36	Tom Taylor	41,42	Robert Fletcher	48
Donald Coy	36	Charles May	42	Philo Lund	48
Winslow Brooks	36	Carl Schroeder	42	Fred Mitchell	48
Earl Schenck	37,38	Dave Roderick	42	Allen Morgan	47,48,49,50
Norm Turay	37,38	Bob Payne	43,46	Roger Baird	49,50,51
John Carey	37,38	Elliott Loken	43	Wilbur Lowe	49,50
Leo Hawel	37,38	Hal Willits	43*	Ken Walters	49,50,51*
Bob Murray	37,38,39	John Dresslar	43	Roy Putnam	49
Gus Eriksen	37,38	Jack Ervin	43	Don Breitenberg	49
John Rosenkranz	37,38	Art Mortensen	43	Harold Brown	49
Ewen Dingwall	38	Ernie Miller	43	Tren Griffin	49,50,51
George Chicha	38	Wally Soli	43	Al Ulbrickson	50,51,52*
John Gallup	38	Bill Dehn	43	Carl Lovsted	50,51,52
Robert Wescott	38	Grant Bishop	46,47	Warren Helgerson	50
Ted Alderson	38,39	Jim Tupper	46,47	Phil Horrocks	50
Victor Michaelson	38,39,40	Jim Horlsley	46	Dick Jordan	50
Herb Graybeal	38	John Anderson	46,47	Owen Miller	50
Hugh Caldwell	38	Bill Works	46,47,48*	George Weiss	50
Don Thompson	38,40	Dave Thompson	46,47*	Jim Callaghan	51

Jack Fletcher	52	Mick McKeown	57	Steve Grant	62
Bill Cameron	51,53	Lou Gellermann	56,58	Jim Gavin	62,63,64
Eric Fonkalsrud	53	Doug Lusher	56	Jerry Johnsen	62,63,64
Fil Leanderson	52,53*	Charles Bower	56	Lou Dodd	62,64*
Dick Wahlstrom	52,53	Phil Kieburtz	56,57,58	Jon Runstad	62,63,64
Joe McIntyre	51,53	Dick Erickson	56,57,58	Chuck Brayshaw	63
Al Rossi	52,53	Andy Hovland	56,57,58	Tom Mills	63,64
Skip John	52,53	John Fish	57,58	Dick Shindler	63,64
Guy Harper	52,53,54	Ross Holmstrom	57,58	John Baker	64
Keith Riely	52,53,54	John Nordstrom	57,58	Chas Campbell	64
Roland Camfield	52,53	Charles Alm	57,58*	Harry Brown	64,66
Ted Frost	52,53,54*	John Bisset	57,58	Rick Clothier	64,65
Jim Howay	52,53,54	Roger MacDonald	58	Larry Haunreiter	64
Ivar Birkeland	52,53	John Sayre	58	Shannon McCormick	64
Whit Clarke	52	Les Eldridge	57	Bill McGonagal	64
Bob Witter	52,53	John Lind	59	Dan McKenzie	64,65
Bob Rogers	55	Ed McRory	59	Dick Moen	64,65*
Bob Smith	55	Jim Christenson	59	Alden Hanson	64
Dick Lacy	53	Bob Svendsen	58,59*	Earl McFarland	64,65,66
Bud Moore	53,54	Gene Phillips	58	Ken Ness	64
Al Stocker	53,54,55*	Ed Argersinger	59	John Vynne	64*
Don Voris	53,56	Dave Fulton	59,61	David Covey	65,66,67
Hans Backer	54	Dave Kinley	60,61	Don Dysart	65,66,67
Art Hart	54	Bill Leland	61	David Kroger	65,66,67*
Dave Purnell	54,55,56*	John Mills	61	Terril Efird	65,66
Lynn Lamb	54,55,56	Gorham Nicol	59,60,61	Bill Pitlick	65,66
Paul Andonian	54,55,56	Fred Raney	59,60,61	Chuck Schluter	67
Doug French	55	Henry Schmidt	59,60,61*	Doug Neil	68*
Ned Ingham	55,56	Brian Wagar	60,61	Howie Wallace	66,67,68
Ron Wailes, Jr.	55,56	John Wilcox	59,60,61	Doug Wilkey	66,68
Bob Thorstensen	55,56*	Ron Wolfkill	60,61*	Lars Andersen	67,68
Wayne Waters	55,56	John Magnuson	60	Bob Moch	67,68
Doug Wetter	55,56	Bill Flint	60	Fred Mann	68,69
Fred Stoll	55,56	Rich Wiberg	60,61	Glen Bowser	67,68,69
Dick Cathey	55	Chuck Holtz	61,62,64*	Dennis Clarke	67
Jay Decker	55	Dean Boender	62	Rick Cole	67,68,69*
Curt Smith	55	Neal Liden	62	Jim Edwards	69,70
Bob Thomas	55	Dave Amundsen	63*	Larry Johnson	70
Floyd Barker	56*	Mike Duppenthaler	63	Brian Miller	68,69,70
Hal Condon, Jr.	55,56	Grant Allen	62	Brad Thomas	68,69,70
Gene Nommensen	55	John Campbell	62,63	Mike Viereck	68,69,70

Dwight Phillips	69,70,71*	Terry Culbertson	74	William Bothel	76
Chad Rudolph	69,70*	Bill Pearce	74	Steve Sabo	76
Tom Burkhart	70	John Roberts	74	Scott Donaldson	76,77
Mike Buse	70	Craig Rosequist	74	William Miller	76,77
Norm Chiang	70	Denny Steinman	74	Tommy Damm	77
Rich Olson	70	Jim Brinsfield	73,74,75	Rick Robinson	77
Dee Walker	70	George Naden	73,74,75	David Dickhaus	76,77,78
Art Arneson	70	Dwight Roesch	73,74,75*	Paul Quinney	76,77,78
Dave White	69,70,71	Steve Thomson	73,74,75	Don Scales	76,77,78
Greg Nukker	70,71	Degraff Berkey	73,75	Mark Sawyer	76,77,78
Rex Thompson	70,71	Gil Gamble	74,75	John Stillings	77,78*
John Baranski	71	Norm Millar	74,75	Robert Umlauf	77,78
Rich Eng	71	Mike Connolly	74	Rick Kuhns	78
Chuck Knoll	71	Chet Genther	75	Mark Tuller	78
Dick Thompson	71	Stu Ketcham	75	Charles Naden	77
Bill Byrd	70,71,72	Robert Legg	75	Michael Fountain	77,78
Rick Copstead	70,71,72	Mike Morgan	75	Brian Martin	77,78
Cliff Hurn	70,71,72*	Dana Wagner	75	Thomas Bascom	77,78,79
Chas Ruthford	70,71,72*	Chris Allsop	74,75,76	Terry Fisk	77,78,79*
Craig Smith	70	Fred Fox	74,75,76	Mark Miller	77,78,79
Jim Hart	72	Stu Johnson	74,75,76	Rolfe Will	78
Bruce Beall	71,72,73	Mark Olason	74,75,76	Mitchell Silver	78
Jon Buse	71,72,73*	Steve Smith	74,75,76	Lewis Hiatt	78
Fred Schoch	71,72,73	Chris Wells	74,75,76*	Preston Simmons	78
Pete Suni	71,72,73	Carl Coon	75,76	Dale Haak	78
Mike Bronson	71,72,73*	Jim McDougall	75,76	Tim Winston	78
Wes Clingan	72,73	Steve Urback	75,76	Bill Erdly	78
Paul Julien	72,73	Greg Allan	76	Bill Walker	78
Jim Maxwell	72,73	Dan Lewis	75	Tony Parker	78
Bill Mickelson	71,72,73	Jessee Franklin	75,76,77	Mike Pederson	78,79
Norm Green	73	Ron Jackman	75,76,77	David Magee	78,79
Mel Hanson	73	Ross Parker	75,76,77	David Kehoe	78,79
Scott Raaum	73	Mark Umlauf	75,77*	James Shinbo	78,79
David Tennesen	73	Mike Weight	75	Daniel Monte	78,79
Mike Cole	72,73,74*	Bret Barnecut	76,77	Mark Putman	78,79
Tom Henry	72,73,74	Bob Berghuis	76,77	Bill Hubbard	78,79,80
Mark Norelius	72,73,74	Doug Jones	76,77	Greg Giuliani	78,79,80*
Dave Reese	72,73,74	Mitch Millar	76,77	Mark Florer	78,79,80
T. Vanbronkhorst	72,73,74	Skip Keely	77	Keith Yasutake	78,79,80
Tom Giovanelli	73,74	Michael Hess	75,77,78*	Paul Barker	78,79,80
Andy Barker	74	Kris Schoenberg	75,77,78	John Wunsch	79

Randy Baze	80	David Lauber	81	Ed Ives	81,83
Uglesa Janjic	79	John Christianson	81	Blair Horn	81,82,83*
Scott Carter	79,80	Brad Schock	81	Charles Van Pelt	81,83
Mark Peterson	79,80	Marius Felix	79,80,82*	Todd Landwehr	82,83
Jim Pugel	79,80	Eric Cohen	80,81,82*	Lee Miller	82,83
Tim Welsh	79,80	Gary Dohrn	80,81,82	Robert Anderson	83
Brock Adler	80	Alan Erickson	80,81,82	Willis Black	83
Ross Gilmour	80	Alan Forney	80,81,82	Regan Brossard	83
John Menefee	80	Nebojsa Janjic	80,82	Dale Holdren	83
Joe Towner	80	Greg Hoffman	81,82	Howard Lee	83
Charles Clapp	79,80,81	Guy Lawrence	81,82	Tom Lee	83
Frank Davidson	79,80,81	Kevin Hansen	82	Jim Lovsted	83
Gary Evans	79,80,81	Robert Schwartz	82	Pat O'Connel	83
Eric Watne	79,80,81*	Sam Eastabrooks	81,82,83	Dave Querubin	83
John Zevenbergen	79,80,81				

IRA winners, 1970. From left: Jim Edwards, coxswain; Cliff Hurn, stroke; Rick Copstead; Mike Viereck; Chad Rudolph; Brian Miller; Brad Thomas; Larry Johnson; Greg Miller, bow

Appendix C

W OMEN'S INTERCOLLEGIATE rowing was established as a major sport at the University of Washington in 1976. The following is a complete list of "Big W" letter-winners from that time through 1983.

Kristen Bolland	76	Linda Cox	76,77,78	Mary Hartman	79,80
Rebecca Fairchild	76	Kay Cockrell	77,78	Andrea Flint	79,80
Laraine Michalson	76	Carol Lake	77,78	Kathleen Tyler	79,80
Barbara Mitchell	76	Di Schueler	77,78	Marilyn Magnuson	79,80
Siri Moss	76	Judy Schwanki	77,78	Jill Duncan	80,81
Carolyn Patton	76	Lisa Drumheller	78	Lori Slehofer	79,80,81
Lucy Rochester	76	Lynn Armstrong	79,80	Lynn Athmann	80,81
Gail Schueler	76	Jane Clark	79	Susan Broome	80,81,82
Marian Small	76	Laura Jackson	78,79	Jill Esterly	80,81
Jo Smart	76	Julianna Jones	79	Madeline Hanson	80,81,82
Cynthia Ziobron	76	Elizabeth Mayer	78,79	Jane McDougall	80,81,82
Ellen Bascom	76,77	Debora Mayer	79	Shyril O'Steen	80,81
Laura Leigh Brakke	76,77	Molly McDonald	79	Mary Silrum	80
Cheryl Kast	76,77	Kathryn Rousso	78,79	Cynthia Spranger	80,81
Laura McDougall	76,77	Jeanne Bulger	77,78,79,80	Sharon Walker	80
Janet McPherson	76,77	Cynthia Wilson	77,78,79	Peg Achterman	81,82
Suzanne Smith	76,77	Gayle Graves	78,79	Penny Craig	81
Teresa Steed	76,77	Karla Godwin	78,79,80,81	Sharon Ellzey	81,82
Sue Beal	77	Kathy Hamlin	78,79,81	Tracy Hearing	81
Lisa Black	77	Lisa Miller	78,79,80	Lisa Horn	81,82
Angella Carbonotto	77	Mary Stoertz	78,79	Monica Kronlof	81,82
Kathy Bulger	76,77,78	Becky Fairchild	78,79	Nancy Leppink	81
Jane Clark	76,77,78	Laurie Dion	79,80	Martha Miller	81

Debbie Moore	81,82	Candace Fullerton	83	Julie Shemeta	83
Kathleen Morris	81	Janise Fulton	82,83	Laura Smith	83
Kristi Norelius	81,82	Maureen King	83	Loren Smith	82,83
Susan Storey	81	Karen Mohling	81,82,83	Marisa Velling	81,82,83
Margie Cate	82	Ellen Pottmeyer	81,82,83	Susan Winters	81,82,83
Julie Baker	82,83				

Appendix D

The following is believed to be a complete list of University of Washington crew alumni who became rowing coaches at universities across the United States.

Ed Leader, Washington, Yale

Rusty Callow, Washington, Penn, Navy

Ky Ebright, California

Russ Nagler, California

Don Grant, Yale

Fred Spuhn, Princeton

Jim Matthews, Penn

Al Ulbrickson, Washington

Stork Sanford, Cornell

Norm Sonju, Cornell, Wisconsin

Tom Bolles, Washington, Harvard

Ellis MacDonald, Marietta

Charles Logg, Rutgers

Loren Schoel, Syracuse, Cornell, Marietta

Harvey Love, Harvard

Walt Raney, Washington, Columbia

Bob Moch, Washington, MIT

Jim McMillin, MIT

Delos Schoch, Princeton

Gene Melder, Clark

Mike Murphy, Wisconsin

Gosta Ericksen, Washington, Syracuse

Fil Leanderson, Washington and MIT

* Dick Erickson, MIT, Washington

John Bisset, Washington, UCLA

Vic Michaelson, Brown, Syracuse

Charles Jackson, Washington, MIT

Stan Pocock, Washington

*Rick Clothier, Washington, Navy

John Lind, Washington, Loyola

Doug Neil, Cornell, Wisconsin

Al Stocker, Western Washington

Ron Wailes, Yale

Lou Gellermann, Washington, Navy

Bob Diehl, Western Washington

Jerry Johnson, UCLA

*Bruce Beall, Harvard and MIT

*Fred Schoch, Harvard, Navy

*Chris Allsop, New Hampshire

*Gil Gamble, Washington

* Presently coaching (1986)

170

Bibliography

A PARTIAL LISTING of sources available to those readers whose interest in George Pocock and the sport of rowing prompts further research:

Official Records

American Rowing Association
Intercollegiate Rowing Association
National Association of Amateur Oarsmen
Pacific Coast Conference Records Books

Articles

Pocock, George, and Clarence Dirks. "One-Man Navy Yard." *Saturday Evening Post* 210 (June 25, 1938), 16–17, 43–49.

Scherck, G. "University of Washington, Cradle of Rowing Coaches." *Sunset* 55 (July 1925), 20–21, 54–55.

Ulbrickson, Alvin, and Clarence Dirks. "Rockne of Rowing." *Saturday Evening Post* 209 (June 19, 1937), 14, 93–97.

"The Washington Huskies." *Life* 26 (June 20, 1949), 39–42.

Mendenhall, Thomas C. "Hiram Conibear." *The Oarsman* 10:5 (Sept./Oct. 1978), 22–29.

——— "The Pococks." *The Oarsman* 13:2 (April/May 1981), 8–12.

Books

Glendon, Richard A., and Richard J. Glendon. *Rowing*. Philadelphia: J. B. Lippincott, 1923.

Johnson, Robert B. *A History of Rowing in America*. Milwaukee: Corbitt and Johnson, 1871.

Kelley, Robert F. *American Rowing*. New York: G. P. Putnam's Sons, 1932.

Newell, Gordon. *H. W. McCurdy Marine History of the Pacific Northwest*. 1966, 1976.

Theses

Torney, John A. "A History of Competitive Rowing in Colleges and Universities of the United States of America," Ed.D., Teachers College, Columbia University, 1958.

Ulbrickson, Alvin Edmund. "The History of Intercollegiate Rowing at the University of Washington through 1963," Master's Thesis, University of Washington, 1963.

Northam, Janet Anne. "Sport and Urban Boosterism: Seattle, 1890–1910," Master's Thesis, University of Washington, 1978.

Index

Boldface numbers refer to photographs.

Aarr, Arthur, 36
Adam, Gordon B., 102
Adams, Clyde, 40
Alaska-Yukon-Pacific Exposition, 38, 139
Alm, Chuck, 86
America, steamship, 115
Anderson, Marian, 85

Baird, Roger, 124
Barret, "Bosh," 111
Barry, Ernest, 12, 117
Beck, Brous, 36
Belford, J. G., 147
Beresford, Jack, 21
Berlin Olympics, 9, 100–4, 108
Bishop, Grant, 115
Bisset, John, 86
Blethen, Alden J., 79
Blethen, Frank, 140
Boeing, W. E., 52, 54, 57, 58, 60–63, 74
Boeing Airplane Co., 53, 55, 60–62, 65, 70, 88, 93
Bolles, Tom, 101, 132, 133, 140
Boston Globe, 89

Bowen, Gil, 136
Bowton, John, 14
Britannia, shell, 19
Brokaw, Clyde, 46
Brougham, Royal, 80, 100, 107, 151
Brunswick, Bob, 148
Bullock, Edith, 69
Burk, Joe, 98, 99
Burns, Kenneth J., 16
Burns, Rev. Robert, 127, 128

Callaghan, Jim, 124
Callow, Gordon, 69, 88
Callow, Robert, 69
Callow, Russell ("Rusty"), 43, 46, 51, 63, 66–70, 68, 72–74, 76, 77, 79, 80, 83, 88, 89, 93, 97, 121, 131, 132, 135, 144
Callow, Dr. Ted, 69
Cambridge University, 8, 124
Cameron, Bill, 124
Campbell, A. C., 43
Campbell, Arthur, 43, 51
Casco, schooner, 48
Churchill, E. L., 20
Clipper Too, 4-oared shell, 116
Colbert, George, 7

Coles, Billy, 14
Collyer, John L., 80
Condon, Harold, 140
Conibear, Hiram, 32, 33–51 *passim,* 41, 76, 80, 136, 141, 144
Conibear, Katherine, 70, 71
Cook, Bob, 3
Courtney, Charles, 74

Davenport, Horace, 80
Day, Charles, 102
Deusen, Denny, 148
Dobie, Gilmour, 48, 49
Doggett, Thomas, 15, 16
Doggett's Coat & Badge, 15, 16, 28
Donaldson, Jim, 83
Dutton, Harry John, 72

Ebright, Carroll M. ("Ky"), 114, 115, 117, 133–34, 135, 137
Eden, Anthony, 19, 129
Edward VII, 18, 109
Edwards, Jim, 167
Erickson, Dick, 82, 86, 133, 134, 152
Erickson, Gus, 133, 139

Eton College, 5, 8, 9, 10, 19, 84, 109–12
Eton on Thames, 9, 15, 18, 109
Everest, H. P., 150

Farwell, Ray, Jr., 151
Fletcher, Jack, 124
Foley, Jim, 54, 55
Frankland, Jim, 46
Frye Packing Co., 43

Gellermann, Lou, 86
George Pocock, shell, 158
Gertrude Sharlotte, shell, 14
Ginger, John, 136
Giovanelli, Gordon, 117
Glendon, Dick, 74, 134, 144
Glerup, Marius, 140
Goertz, Fred, 25
Goes, Clifford ("Tip"), 80, 127
Golden State, motor vessel, 118
Goodsell, Major, 113
Gott, Edgar, 62
Grace, Princess, 143
Green, Tommy, 13
Grisdale, Bill, 69
Gurenna, Husky, 54

Haldane, J. B. S., 19
Hammer, Paul, 43, 46
Harding, Charles, 14
Harr, Adolph ("Short"), 46
Harris, Curly, 136
Hart, Jim, 140
Helms Rowing Hall of Fame, 151
Henley on Thames, 12, 98
Henley Regatta, 84, 86, 104, 114, 115, 139
Herrick, Robert, 80
Higinson, Francis Lee, 80
Hitler, Adolf, 104–107
Hitler Youth, 104
Holt's War Punt, shell, 19
Hovland, Andy, 86
Huckle, Dan, 90
Huckle, George, 57, 90

Hume, Donald B., 102, 106, 107
Hunt, George E., 102
Hunter S. Marston Boathouse, 82
Husky, shell, 70, 74
Husky Clipper, shell, 102, 104, 107, 137, 139
Hutton, George W., 43
Hutton, Will, 43

Isaacs, Walter, 149

Jaroszewiz, Ted, 158
Johnson, Larry, 167

Kearns, Homer, 140
Kearny, Joe, 152
Keeley, Dave, 48
Kelly, Jack, 34, 142, 143
Kelly, Jack, Jr., 143
Kelowna, B.C., 31
Kieburtz, Phil, 86
Kingston on Thames, 5
Kirby, Homer, 36
Kirschner, Harry, 148
Koskela, Norman, 148
Kumm, Ward, 46

Lake Washington Rowing Club, 129
Lakin, Sir Francis, M.D., 109
Langlie, Gov. Arthur B., 150
Lantz, Clint, 35
Laudan, Fred, 149
Leader, Ed, 43, 63, 88, 135, 136
Leader, Elmer, 43
Leanderson, Fil, 122, 133
Lee, Hilmar, 57, 89, 90, 145
Lee, Wilson, 43
Lehmann, Rudy, 3
Lincoln Park Boat Club, 70
Lipton, Sir Thomas, 41
Literary Digest, 73
Livingston, Dr. David, 8
Logan, Ben, 111
Logg, Charles, 122
Logg, Charles, Jr., 123, 139
London Daily Mail, 18

Lovejoy, Bart, 36
Lovsted, Carl, 122, 124
Lowry, Doak, 36
Luckenbach Steamship Co., 73

MacDonald, Ellis, 139
MacNaught, Malcolm, 90
Manhattan, steamship, 101, 102
Marlow Rowing Club, 115
Maroney, Terah, 53
Marston, Hunter S., 84
Martin, Glenn L., 53
Martin, Robert G., 117
Matthews, Jim, 140
May, Charles, 132
McConihe, Paul, 43, 46
McCurdy, H. W., 5, 50, 51, 80, 92, 132, 151, 152
McCurdy, Tom, 92, 151
McElmon, Fred, 35
McIntyre, Joe, 124
McIntyre, Scott, 153
McMillin, James B., 102, 139
Melder, Gene, 139
Michaelson, Vic, 83, 84, 139
Middleton, Keith, 71
Miller, Brian, 167
Miller, Greg, 167
Mjorud, Herb, 136
Moch, Robert G., 102, 105–7, 133, 137–39, 151
Morgan, Allen, 117
Morris, Don, 136
Morris, Roger, 102
Morse, Ray, 131
Murphy, Mike, 139

National Rowing Foundation, 151
New York Times, 97, 100, 157
New York World-Telegram, 100
Nickalls, Guy, 3
Nitzell, Gunnar, 118, 121
Norman, Don, 148
Norman, Jerry, 148

O'Brien, F. L., 36
O'Neal, Arthur, 36
Ottrey, Grace, 110, 112, 114

Ottrey, James, 21, 54, 110, 112, 114
Owens, Jim, 133
Oxford University, 8, 124

Pack, Rev. Paul, 149, 151
Parrott, Gordon, 136
Pay Streak, shell, 139
Phillips, Alton, 136
Phillips, Gene, 86
Plaisted, Fred A., 142
Pocock, Aaron, 4, **5,** 6, 9, 10, 12, 14, 15, **16,** 18, 20, 23, 39, 41, 42, 84, 109, 112
Pocock, Chris, 148
Pocock, Dick, 3, 6, 13–15, **16,** 18–63 *passim,* **56, 57**
Pocock, Frances, 6, 63, **64,** 66, 74, 91, 107, 111, 114, 118, **120,** 123, 127
Pocock, Fred, 6
Pocock, Julia, 6, 18
Pocock, Kathleen, 6, 18, 39, 42, 48
Pocock, Lucy, 6, 15, **17,** 20, 39, 42, 48, 63
Pocock, Patricia May (Mrs. Edward Van Mason), 91
Pocock, Stan, 91, 123, 125, 129, **130, 131,** 133, **148, 150,** 154
Pocock, Thomas, 8
Pocock, William, 8
Porter, Bob, 6
Poughkeepsie, N.Y., 42, 43, 63, 70, 71, 74, 75, 141
Poughkeepsie Regatta, 100, 131
Prajadipok, Prince, 19
Price, Gladys, 127, 128
Price, Keith, 127, 128
Price, Tom, 123
Pullen, Dan, **35**

Rados, Mike, 148
Raetzloff, Dan, 148
Raney, Bud, 133, 139
Rantz, Joseph, 102

Rathe, Gary, 148
Read, Frank, 125
Reichs Sports Stadium, 105
Rice, Jim, 74
Rickenbacker, Capt. Eddie, 62, 63
Rodgers, shell, 42
Roosevelt, Theodore, 142
Rose, John, **153**
Rossi, Al, **122**
Rudolph, Chad, **167**
Runnymede, 18
Russell, Eugene H., 95

Sanford, Harrison ("Stork"), 72, 113, 139, **140**
Sayre, John, **86**
Schmidt, Henry, **136**
Schoch, Dutch, 139
Schoel, Loren, **83,** 139
Seattle, motor vessel, 118
Seattle Post-Intelligencer, 65, 80, 100, 107, 151
Seattle Spirit, shell, 46
Seattle Spirit II, shell, 46
Seattle Times, 76, 79, 95, 113
Shepperton on Thames, 8, 9
Shoudy, Dr. Loyal, 73, 80
Smith, Franklin ("Pat"), **153**
Sonju, Norman, 113, 139, **140,** 141
Sopwith, Tom, 54
Spirit of Tom McCurdy, shell, 151, 152
Sports Illustrated, 152
The Sportsman, 14
Stanley, H. M., 7, 8
Stevenson, Robert Louis, 18
Stimson, Jim, 80
Stoke Poges, 18
Strauss, Dr. Alfred, 70, 147
Suzzallo, Dr. Henry, 48, 49, 51, 52, 63
Svendsen, Bob, **86**

Taylor, Ed, 43
Ten Eyck, Jim, 74, 141, 144

Terry, Lawrence, 105
Thomas, Brad, **167**
Thomsen, Ev, **36**
Tokyo Tea Room, **38,** 46, 65
Tom McCurdy, shell, 92
Totem, shell, 97
Troy, Mayor Peter, 71
Tunisian, steamship, 20, 22, 23
Tupper, Jim, 115
Turner, Charles, 90

Ulbrickson, Al, 99–101, **103,** 106–10, 112, 114, 132, 133, **137, 140,** 149, 151, 156
Ulbrickson, Al, Jr., **122,** 124

Vail, Dan, 74
Vancouver, B.C., 20, 23–25, 42
Vancouver Rowing Club, 26, 27, 28, 34, 42, 125
Van Kuran, Carl, **35**
Van Mason, Ed, 148
Van Winkle, Rick, 148
Varnell, George, 79, 101, 113
Vesper Rowing Club, 129
Vicars, Lucy, 6
Victor Spencer, shell, 125
Victoria I, shell, 18
Viereck, Mike, 167

Wahlstrom, Dick, 122
Wallace, William N., 157
Waller, Harold, 46
Wallis, Ben, 54, 134
Walsh, Buck, 131, 132, 142–44
Walske, Max, 43
Walters, Ken, 124
Ward, Arthur ("Stub"), 46
Watson, Rolfe, 153
Watts, Margaret, 6
Way, Walter, 70
Westerveldt, Conrad, 53
Westland, Warren D., 116, 117

Westminster College, 8
White, John G., 102
Will, Clark, 43
Will, Robert J., 116, 117
Williams, Joe, 100
Williamson, Don, 136
Willis, Hart, 36

Windsor, 9, 18, 109, 110
Windsor, "Froggy," 111
Witter, Dean, 80
Wood, Mervin, 127
Wood, Mrs. Mervin, 127
Woodward, Reggie, 126
Worden, William, 152

Wray, Jim, 144
Wuthenow, Arthur, 140
Wykoff, Halsey, 72, 73

Young, Charles, 20

Zimmerman, Heine, 43,
    46

The Washington-California freshman race, Sheridan Beach, 1940